vines

buyer's guide to canadian wine
vines

by Walter Sendzik with Christopher Waters

whitecap
Vancouver/Toronto

The information in this book is true and complete to the best of our knowledge.
All recommendations are made without guarantee on the part of the author
or Whitecap Books Ltd. The author and publisher disclaim any liability in
connection with the use of this information. For additional information,
please contact Whitecap Books Ltd., 351 Lynn Avenue, North Vancouver,
BC V7J 2C4

Visit our web site at www.whitecap.ca

Edited by Carolyn Bateman
Proofread by Ann-Marie Metten
Cover design by Maxine Lea
Art direction by Roberta Batchelor
Interior design by Margaret Lee / Bamboo & Silk Design Inc.
Cover photograph by Stephen Wolf / firstlight.ca

Printed and bound in Canada

National Library of Canada Cataloguing in Publication Data
Main entry under title:
   Vines buyer's guide to Canadian wines

   ISBN 1-55285-278-4

   1. Wine and wine making—Canada. I. Sendzik, Walter, 1972-
II. Title: Vines (St. Catharines, Ont.)
TP559.C3V548 2001   641.2'2'0971   C2001-910988-1

The publisher acknowledges the support of the Canada Council for the Arts
and the Cultural Services Branch of the Government of British Columbia for our
publishing program. We acknowledge the financial support of the Government
of Canada through the Book Publishing Industry Development Program for our
publishing activities.

For a free copy of *Vines* magazine,
contact us at 1-888-883-3372.

CONTENTS

FOREWORD

My wine education began in the back of the Blue Rodeo tour bus, sipping first-growth Bordeaux, Italian Barolos, Brunello di Montalcino and big beefy California Cabernets —all from Styrofoam cups. We truly had no idea what we were doing, except for what we read in magazines and heard through word of mouth. Humble beginnings but still enough to pick up the prevailing wine elitism that was so common in the '80s and '90s.

It seemed that to become knowledgeable about wine, all you needed to do was try all the most written- and talked-about wines. Somewhere in the process of accomplishing this, I began to realize how little I knew and how much I was missing in the world of wine. Once you visit a region, meet the people who make and drink the local product and take in the surroundings from the air to the soil, you begin to see that only part of the story is ever written in the wine magazines. The rest is up to you to discover.

A couple of years ago my wife, Rena, and I made a discovery of our own. Having lived in Toronto for many years, we had somehow never ventured far enough into Niagara. When the chance arose to tour the wineries there, we took it up not knowing what to expect. The first stunning moment was our first view of the vineyards. We had no idea the land was so beautiful. The soft rolling hills, the green valleys and the sweet smell of the air were quite simply beautiful. Next we saw the grand wineries, the cozy tasting rooms and the barrel cellars; we just couldn't believe we were in Ontario.

Then we made our most startling discovery of the tour—the winemakers. The folks who make wine in Canada are as charismatic, poetic, funny and talented as any I have met in the world. At the beautiful and historic Inniskillin Winery, we met Donald Ziraldo. He's classy and irreverent and can tell you the history of the Canadian wine industry with such charm you just can't get enough. We tasted many fine wines, but the one that stands out for me was the barrel sample of the '98 Founders' Reserve Pinot Noir. This wine had depth and nuance and it was still in short pants, as they say in the business.

Across the peninsula, in the village of Jordan, we met Angelo Pavan, winemaker of Cave Spring Cellars, who also happens to be a former philosophy major. We tasted many crisp Rieslings and Chardonnays, and we left having bought enough cases of their '97 Riesling to supply my brother's wedding. Our journey ended at the picturesque Vineland Estates with a dinner overlooking the vineyards. We were joined by winemaker Brian Schmidt, who enlightened us about the experimentation and tinkering that goes into making a fine Meritage. And fine it was; we sipped as the sun went down on the beautiful sheltered hamlets of the Niagara wine region. The perfect end to a great day!

Later that same year I had the good fortune to be playing in Kelowna, British Columbia. Having read about the Okanagan Valley as an emerging wine region on the international scene, I decided to use some free time to taste some of the local wines. Almost across the road from the Grand Hotel, where we were staying, I paid a visit to one of B.C.'s oldest wineries, Calona Wines, in the heart of Kelowna. I had the privilege of meeting with winemaker Howard Soon. We tasted, talked, ate and tasted again. I left with a great memory of sweet, dusty Pinot Noirs and peachy, glycerine-style Chardonnays. Leaving the city, and remembering what Soon had said about the depth and quality of the wine industry, I marvelled at the backdrop of majestic mountains with vineyards rolling up the slopes from Okanagan Lake.

As Donald Ziraldo once suggested, the wine industry bears a resemblance to the Canadian music industry of the 1980s when performers like Cowboy Junkies, Tragically Hip, Blue Rodeo and k.d. lang were first hitting the scene. The music had been percolating for a few years and was on the verge of breaking. Many people knew the quality of these bands, but many more did not. It took a few breaks, some loyal fans and support from radio to make it bust out. When it did, it was the good music that carried our little music scene to the rest of the world. The wine industry in this country is at the same crossroads. Many know the numerous fine wines produced in Canada, but too many do not. It's all there waiting for discovery— the characters, the land and the wines. This book will be a helpful roadmap on your journey to discovering the wines of Canada. Enjoy.

Jim Cuddy
Toronto, 2001

ACKNOWLEDGMENTS

First, to all the panel members who graciously donated their time to taste a lot of wine. To Marcus Ansems, Anna Ananicz, Peter Bailey, James Bertrand, Dr. Linda Bramble, Laurie Clark, Ray Cornell, Roberto DeDomenico, Dr. Ramon de Miro Orduna, Janet Dorozynski, Sigrid S. Gertsen-Briand, Vic Harradine, Wendy Hunt, Jeff Innes, Tim Kerr, Tammy Kruk, Steven Page, Angelo Pavan, Terry Petherick, Dr. Rod Phillips, Dr. Gary Pickering, Johannes Reinhart, Carolyn Ricketts, Steven Sokolowski, Sue-Ann Staff, Joe Will and Roger Stefan Wills for all of the comments, notes and general discussions about the wine. Without all your valuable input, this book would be a shell of what it is.

To Jim Cuddy for writing the foreword to this book. Since meeting you way back in the early days when we went on that wonderful tour of Niagara, you've been very generous in helping the magazine by lending us your wine wisdom and notable name. Looking forward to more evenings under the stars trying to come up with eclectic descriptions of wines.

To Marissa D'Onofrio for pouring so much wine. As principal researcher of this project, you did everything from collecting wine labels to phoning wineries for prices. Your diligence and attention to detail was invaluable as we headed down the final stretch. A big thanks for saving us so much time.

To Bremner Biscuit Company from Denver, Colorado, for believing in a book about Canadian wines enough to supply all the panel tastings with crackers. Hailed as the perfect match for wine tasting because of their flavourless profile, the crackers were indeed an ideal match.

The Vintage Niagara Adventures and Tammy Kruk for providing bottle wraps for all the tastings. With the use of the convenient bottle wraps, VNA ensured that all tastings were blind. Big time savers, they were very valuable to the tastings. Check out the web site at www.vna.on.ca for more information on bottle wraps.

Further thanks to the awesome people at Whitecap Books for their strong commitment to ensuring that this pioneering book made it to print. To Robert McCullough for believing enough in Canadian wines to publish a buyer's guide on it. To Alison Maclean, Mike White, Robin Rivers and Angela Roberge for words of encouragement and strong convictions in getting the book from an idea to reality.

To all those who have supported the idea that a book like this could be produced—my lovely wife Melanie Sendzik, Mom and Dad Sendzik, Pat Waters, Ali Waters and the rest of the Sendzik and Waters clan, we extend a big hug and thanks for putting up with all those weekends spent tasting wine and those endlessly long nights writing the book. A special thanks to Scully from Walter for her ability to nudge and tug at just the right moment.

Finally, but certainly not least, we would like to acknowledge those in the Canadian wine industry who have supported *Vines Magazine* since our early years. *Vines* is a creation of your years of hard work. If it were not for the great number of hardworking winemakers and entrepreneurs who have taken the Canadian wine industry to new heights, this book could not have been completed. This buyer's guide is testimony to all of your tireless efforts to make great wine—wine that all Canadians can be proud of.

By purchasing this book, you will be showing your support of products that are 100 percent Canadian. Consider buying another one; it would make a great stocking stuffer or birthday gift for the wine enthusiasts on your list.

INTRODUCTION

Last year, *Vines* magazine published a special issue dedicated to buying Canadian wine, the first of its kind produced in Canada. For our main article, we tasted 325 wines and rated and ranked the best of the bunch. It turned out to be one of our best-selling issues to date. The response was immediate and overwhelming. For months following that issue's release, consumers and producers alike asked about the possibility of publishing a more comprehensive consumer's guide to the wines of Canada. With well over a hundred commercial wineries producing 100 percent Canadian wine, we looked at the large number of wines being produced and decided it was a very real possibility. Samples were solicited, organized and put to a panel of experts and wine lovers. This panel discussed the merits of each wine and ranked them accordingly. Now, almost a year to the date of the release of that special consumer's guide issue, we offer our expansive *Vines Buyer's Guide to Canadian Wine.*

Looking back over the history of Canadian wines, we note that it's been only in the past 25 years that wine-makers began to focus on producing quality, European-styled, vinifera wines. Sure, back in the '60s and '70s, Canadian wineries produced blended table wine and a lot of "pop" wines, which sold very well, but a shift took place in the Canadian wine industry in the mid-70s that revolutionized the quality of Canadian wines.

Led by risk-takers like Karl Kaiser and Donald Ziraldo (who opened Inniskillin, Canada's first estate winery in 1975), Paul Bosc Sr. of Château des Charmes and Joe Pohorly, founder of Newark Winery (which would become Hillebrand Estates Winery after he sold it), the industry started to focus on producing varietal wines from French hybrid and European vinifera grapes. In British Columbia, that pioneering spirit was furthered by Harry McWatters from Sumac Ridge Estate Winery, George Heiss of Gray Monk Cellars and Bob and Lee Claremont, who opened the first estate winery in British Columbia—the now-defunct Claremont—in 1979.

These visionaries had the nerve and the commitment to challenge the status quo. Although many doubted their collective belief that classical vinifera vines like Chardonnay, Riesling, Cabernet Franc and Merlot could be successfully planted in certain areas of Canada, these pioneers went out and proved that Canada could very well sustain and produce quality grapes, especially in Niagara and the Okanagan Valley. These were planted along with French hybrids like Vidal, Baco Noir and Maréchal Foch, and by the early 1980s a small number of wineries were crafting surprisingly well-made wines.

After demonstrating that the fertile soils and climate conditions of southern Ontario and the Okanagan Valley could yield consistent vinifera wines, a second wave of winemakers emerged in the 1980s. Producers such as Colio Wines, Cave Spring Cellars, Pelee Island Winery, Reif Estate Winery and Vineland Estates in Ontario and Calona Wines, Gehringer Brothers and Quails' Gate in B.C. gave the fledgling industry an extra boost.

These vintners went on to inspire a wave of quality-minded artisan wineries. Some of these include amateur-turned-pro operations Marynissen Estates and Lakeview Cellars in Niagara as well as farm-gate producers Henry of Pelham Family Estate Winery and Pillitteri Estates in Niagara and Blue Mountain Vineyard and Cellars, St. Hubertus Vineyard and Wild Goose Vineyards in the Okanagan Valley.

Much of the activity in the late 1980s and early 1990s was inspired by NAFTA (the North American Free Trade Agreement) as well as the founding of the Vintners' Quality Alliance, first in Ontario in 1989, then in B.C. in 1990. The spectre of a flood of bulk jug wine from California pouring into Canada led domestic wineries to ratchet up the quality of the wine they were producing so they could establish their own niche at the nation's liquor stores.

Instituting winemaking standards through the VQA, which represents the best Canada has to offer in the way of domestic wine, helped achieve that goal. It was a pivotal move taken by the industry to ensure the quality of the wines being produced. It brought the wineries in British Columbia and in Ontario together, working to promote Canadian wines at a time when many people didn't believe in the wines. There are also many quality-minded wineries operating outside of the VQA that focus their production on 100 percent Product of Canada.

The latest surge is a wave of super-premium producers, wineries like Burrowing Owl Vineyards, CedarCreek Estate Winery and Paradise Ranch Winery in B.C. and Creekside Estate, Daniel Lenko Estate Winery, The Malivoire Wine Company, Thirty Bench Vineyard and Thirteenth Street Wine Company in Niagara. All are looking to hit a high note with quality vintages made with low yields of carefully farmed fruit.

The climate is ripe for this buyer's guide. With Canadian wineries routinely bringing home top awards from international competitions, the quality of domestic wine has never been better. Unfortunately, consumer support for Canadian wine across the country hasn't kept pace. Certainly Icewine is always going to be the specialty item that carries the banner for Canadian wineries into the international arena, but there's more to the industry than just sweet dessert wines. Canadian table whites are snapping up medals at VinItaly, the International Wine and Spirit Competition in London, England, and other prestigious, world-class wine events. Our reds are beginning to stand shoulder to shoulder with well-known reds from California, Australia and Europe. And yet, consumers are still reluctant to buy Canadian wines.

We believe that reluctance to buy Canadian comes from an absence of available resources to guide wine consumers through the vast field of wine. Without knowledge of what is being produced and how good it actually is, wine enthusiasts will keep returning to the popular brands that crowd the shelves of liquor stores across Canada. So we designed this book to make it easier for consumers to find, learn about and buy Canadian wines. We've arranged the wines by grape variety or style. If you're a fan of Chardonnay, for example, the Chardonnay section will give you general information about the varietal and how it's produced in Canada. We follow this with an exhaustive review section on Chardonnays made by Canadian wineries starting with the best in the nation and ranking the wines from "Highly Recommended" to "Recommended" and "Quite Good." The same format applies to all widely planted grape varieties. In the case of lesser-known varieties, they have been grouped together for your convenience.

Having tasted more than 1,000 Canadian wines, we've distilled the wide selection down to those that we think you will enjoy—and hopefully come to buy time and again. Many people have said that Canadian wines are one of our best-kept secrets, but we feel it's time to spread the word. Wine is best enjoyed with family and friends. By highlighting these exciting bottles, we welcome you to join in the celebration.

About *Vines* Magazine

Vines magazine grew out of our conviction that there is an audience out there searching for a magazine that explores and celebrates the good life of wine. We believe that the appreciation of wine is part of a multi-dimensional lifestyle. People who drink wine also lead active lives and have a wide variety of other interests, so why should we place wine in a vacuum, isolated from everything else that stimulates and enriches our lives?

We want to put something on the newsstands that clearly says we understand and respect your approach to wine, your knowledge of it and your broad range of experiences with it.

For the past three years, we have been providing readers with a magazine that transcends the staid, pretentious view of wine upheld by other wine publications. We are the first wine magazine in Canada to view wine as part of a lifestyle, not as a hobby or an elite club. Readers have come to understand that with *Vines*, their interest in wine is encouraged to develop through personal experimentation. They are appreciated for their level of wine knowledge, not lectured on it. It's a small but very significant point.

We believed that casual consumers who enjoy a glass of wine would pick up a wine magazine without feeling intimidated if the publication spoke to them. It was an idea that wine can be both entertaining and educational. By placing wine in a cultural context, which includes music, food, art, literature and so much more, we have given readers a larger forum from which they can build their own personal experiences with wine.

And the key element in this tale of a dream reaching fruition is the people behind the conviction. We're not wine snobs—you can trust us on that one. We love wine for what it is—a work of art that conveys stories on so many different levels. For more information on *Vines* magazine, check out our web site at www.vinesmag.com.

How the Reviews Were Created

A collective of people created the reviews for this guide, starting back in February 2001. A wine request fax was sent to all the wineries in British Columbia and Ontario. We asked wineries to submit wines that would be available to the consumer through 2001–02—whether at liquor stores or through wine shops and boutiques. The stipulation was that the wine must be VQA and/or use 100 percent grown-in-Canada grapes. Within weeks, the *Vines* office was flooded with cases of wine. The wine cellar took over the entire basement.

Once all the wines were counted (over a thousand were submitted), we divided up the varieties and began the long process of organizing the panel tastings. Recognizing that everyone has a different palate, we wanted diverse panels that would have different members each time to fully explore the wines. Panels consisted of three to five people. Publisher Walter Sendzik and managing editor Christopher Waters were the regulars while winemakers, wine educators, sommeliers, wine enthusiasts and wine consumers rounded out each panel.

Within their respective groups, we divided the wine by vintage and then by reserve and non-reserve. All tastings were done blind, which means that the panel members knew only the wine type, but not the producer nor the region in which it was produced. This allowed for a great amount of objectivity. Each panel member was directed to score the wines based on the *Vines* magazine five-star rating system. They were also asked to give detailed descriptions of the wine. At the end of each tasting, we collected the tasting sheets, compiled the scores and accorded each wine its ranking.

The difference between reviews in this buyer's guide and others written by wine critics is that these are much more accurate because they are based on a collective resource of information rather than the opinions of just one person.

And finally, Walter Sendzik and Christopher Waters wrote all the reviews. We approached each review with the consumer in mind. Our goal was to educate and entertain. The reviews are a reflection of the wine: the higher the ranking, the more we had to say in the review. And wine is also a part of our culture; we know you'll be able to relate to our cultural references.

Who the Reviewers Are

Marcus Ansems, winemaker, Creekside Estate Winery, Jordan Station

Anna Ananicz, sommelier, St. Catharines

Peter Bailey, editorial page editor, *The Standard*, St. Catharines

James Bertrand, sommelier, director of the National Capital Sommelier Guild, Ottawa

Dr. Linda Bramble, sommelier, wine writer and educator and industry liaison for the Cool Climate Viticulture Institute at Brock University, St. Catharines

Laurie Clark, wine enthusiast, Toronto

Ray Cornell, winemaker, Hernder Estates Winery, St. Catharines

Roberto DeDomenico, winemaker, Reif Estate Winery,
Niagara-on-the-Lake

Dr. Ramon de Miro Orduna, oenologist and sensory
scientist, New Zealand

Janet Dorozynski, Wine and Spirits Education Trust diploma,
Ottawa

Sigrid S. Gertsen-Briand, Lallemand Speciality Fermentation
Products, St. Catharines

Vic Harradine, sommelier, president of the National Capital
Sommelier Guild, director of Algonquin College's
Sommelier Certificate Program

Wendy Hunt, sommelier, The Winery at Peninsula Ridge
Estates Winery, Beamsville

Jeff Innes, winemaker, Harbour Estates Winery, Jordan Station

Tim Kerr, freelance wine writer, Grimsby

Tammy Kruk, president, Vintage Niagara Adventures,
St. Catharines

Steven Page, Barenaked Ladies lead singer and wine lover,
Toronto

Angelo Pavan, winemaker, Cave Spring Cellars, Jordan

Terry Petherick, sommelier, Ottawa

Dr. Rod Phillips, sommelier, Algonquin College Sommelier
Certificate Program instructor, director of the National
Capital Sommelier Guild and author of *A Short History of
Wine* (Penguin UK, 2000), Ottawa

Dr. Gary Pickering, oenologist and sensory scientist,
Cool Climate Viticulture Institute, Brock University,
St. Catharines

Johannes Reinhart, winemaker, Anthony Road Winery,
Finger Lakes, New York

Carolyn Ricketts, wine enthusiast, Toronto

Walter Sendzik, president of Vines Publishing and wine
writer for *Pulse Niagara*, *View* magazine in Hamilton and
Echo, Kitchener-Waterloo, St. Catharines

Steven Sokolowski, wine collector, Toronto

Sue-Ann Staff, winemaker, Pillitteri Estates Winery,
Niagara-on-the-Lake

Christopher Waters, managing editor of *Vines* magazine,
wine columnist and reporter for *The Standard*,
St. Catharines

Joe Will, winemaker and owner, Strewn Wines Inc.,
Niagara-on-the-Lake
Roger Stefan Wills, chef and patron, Café Brussel, Toronto
Bruce Young, wine writer, Lewiston, New York
Jim Warren, consulting winemaker whose clients include
Daniel Lenko Estate Winery and Kacaba Vineyards,
Hamilton

Vines Magazine Rating System

The rating system used for this guide and *Vines* magazine
is based on the five-star rating system. A score is given
only after a thorough, objective assessment of the wine's
qualities. After each panelist submits a rating for the wine,
the ratings are aggregated and the wine is awarded a
ranking within the five-star system.

Vines Award *****

To achieve this ranking, the wine must be of outstanding
quality. The panel awards this mark if the wine is the best of
the tasting. In some cases, the panel decided that the top
wines did not reach a level of superlative quality and there-
fore some sections in the book will not have a *Vines* Award.

Highly Recommended ****

For a wine to achieve this ranking, it must be exceptional.

Recommended ***

These are wines that have some highlighted characteristics.

Quite Good **

These are good, quaffable wines.

Note: Wines that were deemed faulted or not suitable for
recommendation in this guide were not reviewed.

How to Read the Reviews

This is the ranking category

Winery

Vintage and proper
name of wine

Appellation recognized
by the VQA

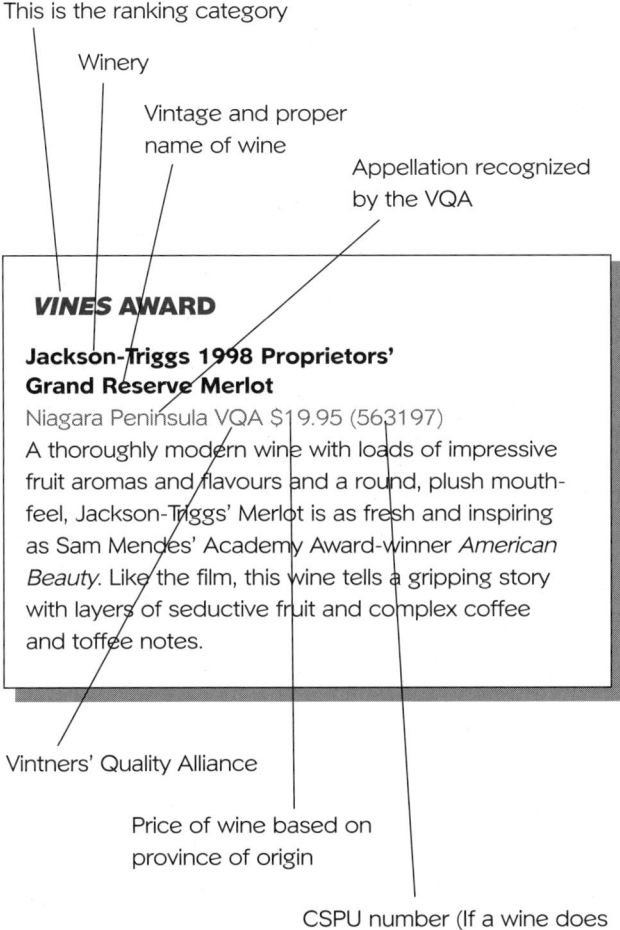

VINES **AWARD**

**Jackson-Triggs 1998 Proprietors'
Grand Reserve Merlot**
Niagara Peninsula VQA $19.95 (563197)
A thoroughly modern wine with loads of impressive
fruit aromas and flavours and a round, plush mouth-
feel, Jackson-Triggs' Merlot is as fresh and inspiring
as Sam Mendes' Academy Award-winner *American
Beauty*. Like the film, this wine tells a gripping story
with layers of seductive fruit and complex coffee
and toffee notes.

Vintners' Quality Alliance

Price of wine based on
province of origin

CSPU number (If a wine does
not have a number, it means it
is sold only at the winery)

WHITE WINE

CHARDONNAY

In the world of wine, Chardonnay remains king. Although waning, its popularity is still such that most wine drinkers think white wine is synonymous with Chardonnay. What's puzzling about its great appeal, however, is that few consumers know what Chardonnay's actual flavour is because the wine is made in such a wide range of styles. Perhaps the root of its allure is its French-bred sophistication; perhaps it is simply that mass-produced Chardonnay is an easy-drinking wine that's smooth and generally straight-forward. Like a Hollywood movie, its in-your-face entertainment washes over you without taxing your facilities too much.

The easy-to-pronounce, easy-to-enjoy white is a delight for all parties concerned—grape grower, winemaker and consumer. The vines flourish in early spring, giving the early ripening variety a head start throughout the growing season.

FOOD PAIRING SUGGESTIONS
Considering the range of Chardonnay styles, there's an equally broad range of potential matches for the wines. Lighter wines are generally more food friendly, while some of the heavily oaked wines require more robust meals to balance the weight and concentrated flavours of the wine. Try dry and delicate *sur lie* wines with oysters and shellfish. Bigger wines can muscle in on salmon, roast chicken and veal.

Once in the winery, Chardonnay is fashioned in a wide range of styles by aging it in oak, on its dead yeast cells or entirely in stainless steel to preserve and focus its fruit flavours. The process greatly affects the flavour, texture and weight of the finished wine. Not all Chardonnays, then, are created equal, which makes labelling terminology all the more crucial to understand.

If you're a fan of crisp and fruity Chardonnays, you're looking to land an unoaked model. The lack of consensus on labelling however means you'll be staring down everything from non-oaked, unoaked or no oak designations. Surely, as you read this, some marketing genius is currently developing "oak free"!

Also on the lighter side, *sur lie* Chardonnays are improved with a lush, creamy texture from the winemaking technique of aging the wine on top of its lees, i.e., yeast cells spent during fermentation. The process also imbues the wine with pleasant nutty and yeasty flavours.

Chardonnays that have seen some oak are generally easier to spot; "barrel aged" or "barrel fermented" will be featured prominently on the label, partially to justify the sticker price. Oak aging, particularly when done in French *barriques*, adds to the expense of the finished wine. Oak aging mellows the fruit and acidity, but if not properly handled, it can overwhelm the positive characteristics and make for a clumsy wine.

The real can of worms in terms of Chardonnay labels is reserve bottles, which are often—but not always—more focused and refined than their barrel-aged brethren. As with other domestic varietal wines, the reserve terminology means essentially whatever the winery wants it to mean. Consumers assume that reserve connotates the vintner's best selection; however, that's not written in stone.

—RD, JI, RP, JR, SS, WS, CW, WH, GP, RdM

VINES AWARD

Chardonnay was the largest and most intensive tasting in this book. With more than 120 entries submitted, selecting the cream of the crop was a daunting task. The range in styles made it especially difficult to pinpoint one wine as the recipient of the *Vines* Award. As the tasting panel's notes were tallied, it was clear there were three favourites that managed to rise above the rest. The scores for all three were identical, yet the descriptions were far from uniform between the trio. So, without further adieu, the award for top Chardonnay goes to …

Burrowing Owl Vineyards 1999 Chardonnay
Okanagan Valley VQA $21.90 (510933)
In recent film history, Mel Gibson's award-winning performance as William Wallace in *Braveheart* captures the expressive character of this wonderful wine. This striking Chardonnay opens with a burst of energized vanilla and banana. With a strong conviction, the wine explodes on the palate with a creamy, flavourful texture that is simply divine. A deft touch of light oak defies the King of Oakland and allows the fruit to ride through to victory. Drinking well now, the mythology of this wine will only get better with age.

Hawthorne Mountain Vineyards 1999 Mountain Reserve Chardonnay
Okanagan Valley VQA $9.95 (576934)
Hawthorne's offering is like Oscar king Tom Hanks. An all-round great wine, this one steals the show with its luscious fruit. Tropical fruits of pineapple, banana and ripe grapefruit are cast away in this sea of Chardonnay. With a little help from some oak, the fruity flavours are balanced with a layer of acidity that drives the wine home. Whether stranded on an island or sitting on a bench with a box of chocolates, this wine will be your bosom buddy.

Pillitteri Estates Winery 1999 Chardonnay Family Reserve
Niagara Peninsula VQA $22.95 (349167)
Pillitteri's Chardonnay weighs in like a Jack LaMotta-style heavyweight. This raging bull earned top marks for its depth and heft. Plump and full of body, the wine opens with a one-two-three punch of buttery popcorn, peach and pear. Oak enters the ring on the palate with a couple of jabs of vanilla and pear. With enough structure and complexity to go the distance, this is one heavyweight champ that could take on many contenders. It will get even better with age.

HIGHLY RECOMMENDED

Cave Spring Cellars 1999 Chardonnay Estate Bottled
Niagara Peninsula VQA $14.95 (471391)
If you're a fan of Chablis-style Chardonnay, you should definitely check this one out. A fruit basket of peaches, pears and apples offers an attractive fragrance to this medium-bodied white. The massive fruit characters continue to impress on the palate with acids creating a warm wrap around the flavours. A hint of buttery oak appears on the finish to cap off this well-made Chardonnay. Built to dwell in the cellar for a while, it can be enjoyed now with light white meat-based dinners or freshwater fish like walleye and perch.

Cave Spring Cellars 1999 Vineyard Chardonnay CSV
Niagara Peninsula VQA $35 (529941)
With enough smoky oak to set off a five-alarm fire, there's plenty of fruit waiting in the wings to take over. After the initial oak rush, lemon and pink grapefruit characteristics emerge. The fruit takes over on the palate and the oak assumes a more supporting role as the wine becomes a web of integrated complexity. Definitely built to age—it's a classic food-pairing wine.

Henry of Pelham Family Estate Winery 1999 Chardonnay Barrel Fermented

Niagara Peninsula VQA $22.95 (268342)

Integration is the key to the success of this wine. Notes of pear and buttery vanilla offer an attractive entry into this deftly oaked Chardonnay. On the palate, toasty oak dominates, but the fruit isn't completely cloaked in it. A layer of acidity allows the fruit to come through on the finish. Although time in the bottle would give this one even more complexity, it would be a nice fit for smoked salmon or roasted chicken.

Hillebrand Estates 1999 Trius Chardonnay Barrel Fermented Lakeshore

Niagara Peninsula VQA $16.95 (291484)

Drinking this wine is like walking into a cedar closet while biting into a Bosc pear. Pleasant aromas of toasted cedar and pear carry over to the palate with a supple richness that gives this wine a good mouth-feel. Loads of fruit and ample oak combine with a streak of soft acids to create a full-bodied Chardonnay with a long finish. This one would be right at home for a holiday turkey dinner.

Inniskillin Wines 1998 Founders' Reserve Chardonnay

Niagara Peninsula VQA $29.95 (529396)

There are no reservations about this reserve Chardonnay. Built like an expensive California-styled reserve, the biggest difference is the price. Affordable and well designed, this one manages to balance the oak with the fruit. Vanilla toasty notes pair well with pear and banana. On the palate, the fruit is upfront with oak rounding out the flavours on the finish. Don't pay more for just oak, when you can get both fruit and oak at a great price.

Malivoire Wine Co. 1999 Chardonnay Moira Vineyard

Niagara Peninsula VQA $35.95 (573154)

This wine captures the essence of an Old World-styled Chardonnay. Like an elder statesman, its big, bold, smoky and gamey notes offer a firm but charismatic welcome. The oak continues to exert its control on the palate with some creamy, butter flavours and some subtle fruit in behind. If you like your Chardonnay with oak, this full-body offering is one for the rack. The complexity of the wine indicates it will age gracefully.

Peninsula Ridge Estates 1999 Chardonnay Barrel Aged

Niagara Peninsula VQA $13.95

Rich, tropical notes of passion fruit, banana and even coconut mingle with a touch of vanilla and almond on the palate. A hot streak on the finish makes this a great match for pork, chicken or shellfish.

Quails' Gate Estate Winery 1998 Chardonnay Family Estate

Okanagan Valley VQA $29.95 (559625)

This lightly oaked Chardonnay allows the fruit to express itself. With hints of lemon and pineapple, the oak doesn't really begin to unfold until the wine hits the palate. The palate is a mix of toast and lemon, making for an interesting, flavourful wine. With a bit of weight, this Chardonnay manages to go the length with a spicy lingering finish. Match with seafood for a pleasurable treat.

Quails' Gate Estate Winery 1999 Chardonnay Limited Release

Okanagan Valley VQA $15.95 (377770)

This wine is worthy of joining the cast of Cirque du Soleil. The luscious pear and almond notes open the show with an incredible balancing act. Citrus flavours join the cast on the palate with another fine balancing act between the oak and soft acids. With its clean, flavour-infused finish, the wine would be a good match for seafood or tossed salad. You get your money's worth with this one.

Vineland Estates 1999 Chardonnay Reserve
Niagara Peninsula VQA $48

A close runner-up to the *Vines* Award, this wine is all about the fruit. Delicious notes of apples and pears make for a mouth-watering hook into the wine. On the palate, toasty vanilla supports the luscious fruit, giving way to a big creamy finish. Harmonious and balanced, this is a reserve from start to finish. Grilled chicken or pork would appreciate a date with this one.

RECOMMENDED

Cave Spring Cellars 1999 Chardonnay Reserve
Niagara Peninsula VQA $19.95 (256552)

This is a Dr. Jekyll and Mr. Hyde type of wine. The bouquet of lemon and green apples indicates a fruit-driven, light-bodied white, but on the palate Mr. Hyde takes over and unleashes a trail of oak. Cedar and pear wrestle for control as a layer of acidity gives the wine a strong character. In the end, Dr. Jekyll's more personable fruit-friendly characteristics seize control, but, with a little aging, Mr. Hyde may appear again.

CedarCreek Estate Winery 1999 Chardonnay
Okanagan Valley VQA $15.95 (237974)

The forecast for this wine calls for a light breeze of lemon and vanilla. This will be followed by a fruity storm bringing heavy doses of pears, apples and pineapple. The downpour will end quickly, giving way to a clear ending to the wine. This soft Chardonnay would be best suited for light meats and green salads.

Cilento Wines 1998 Chardonnay Reserve
Niagara Peninsula VQA $23.95 (510263)
With its bouquet of toast and vanilla, you know
this one has spent some serious time in oak.
Although the oak aging masks the fruit, there's
an attractive vanilla, butterscotch and toffee
profile on the palate. The rich, robust flavours
carry through to a soft and supple finish. Ideal
for heavily aged cheeses and pork dishes.

Hawthorne Mountain Vineyards 1998 Chardonnay
Okanagan Valley VQA $11.75 (440677)
Yell "Timber!" when you uncork this Chardonnay.
Lots of oak on the nose is the first clue that
there's going be some wood action. Yet what
really makes this wine is the fact that the oak isn't
too overpowering; it's more of a buttery vanilla
oak than a harsh, grained oak. On the palate, it's
all vanilla and butterscotch with some soft melon
and pear undertones. A light-to-medium-bodied
white with enough complex flavour profiles to fit
nicely along smoked salmon, grilled veggies and
light white meats.

Inniskillin Wines 1999 Chardonnay Single Vineyard Series, Montague Estate
Niagara Peninsula VQA $16.95 (558015)
The old Bard would appreciate the bountiful fruit
that spills over from this charming single vineyard
wine. Apple blossom and pear give it a youthful
fragrance. On the palate, oak makes a cameo
appearance, but the fruit takes centre stage. If
Romeo had been courting Juliet with this wine in
tow, the Capulets and Montagues would have
become the best of friends.

Inniskillin Okanagan Wines 1999 Chardonnay Reserve
Okanagan Valley VQA $16.95 (558441)

This Chablis-styled Chardonnay focuses on the fruit and uses light contact with oak to round out the body of the wine. Interesting buttery lemon notes give way to more lemon grass flavours on the palate. Some cedar flavours appear on the extended finish. Uncork this one, get your bib on and start cracking open some lobsters.

Kacaba Vineyards 1999 Chardonnay
Niagara Peninsula VQA $21.95

Built for those with a penchant for oak. Lots of smoky bacon and oak with a sprinkle of pear and banana fruit. It's like being in a forest of oak trees with monkeys eating tropical fruit in the trees. Serve with gamey meats, smoked meats and deep-sea fish.

Mission Hill Estate Winery 1999 Chardonnay Private Reserve Bin 99
Okanagan Valley VQA $13.95 (518530)

If you're looking for a Chardonnay without a discernible trace of oak, this is your wine. An expressive fruit cocktail of pineapple, grapefruit, tangerine and lemon smothers the oak and keeps it under wraps from start to finish. A touch of melon sweetness adds to its attractive fruity flavours. Forget the food. Chill and serve as the sun sets.

Mission Hill Estate Winery 1999 Chardonnay Reserve
Okanagan Valley VQA $17.95 (545004)

Following its sibling, this reserve Chardonnay is a basket of bright tropical fruit. Loads of pineapple, apricot and tangerine flavours wash over the palate with a fresh finish. A yummy wine best enjoyed chilled.

Peninsula Ridge Estates 1999 Chardonnay Reserve

Niagara Peninsula VQA $24.95

This Chardonnay is a real charmer. A bouquet of butterscotch and roasted nuts has the brawn and muscle of a big Chard, but the palate reveals a soft and supple side where pears and mangoes hang out and mix it up with the oak. A lingering finish.

Pillitteri Estates Winery 1999 Chardonnay Barrel Aged

Niagara Peninsula VQA $12.95 (349175)

A nice one-two combination of fruit and oak is held together with a streak of sweetness. Toasty vanilla, peaches and pears offer a complex profile for this well-made Chardonnay. Oak and fruit linger on the finish. If you're ordering Chinese food, this one should cover the range of dishes; just make sure to order MSG-free.

Quails' Gate Estate Winery 1998 Chardonnay

Okanagan Valley VQA $15.95 (377770)

Intense straw notes capture the essence of this wine. The straw profile continues to dominate on the palate with some sweet green tea flavours helping the cause. A light offering, its lingering, slightly spicy finish caps a fine wine.

Southbrook Winery 1999 Chardonnay Lailey Vineyard

Niagara Peninsula VQA $19.95 (448316)

According to the dictionary, elegant is defined as gracefully refined; neatly and beautifully made or constructed. This is a fitting definition for this Chardonnay. A subtle fragrance of vanilla and pear gives way to finely integrated oak and fruit on the palate. The oak gives the wine a rounded mouth-feel with the fruit adding a graceful layer that carries the wine through the finish. Not too bold and not too light, this wine is just right.

Strewn Wines 1999 Terroir Chardonnay Strewn Vineyard

Niagara Peninsula VQA $18.95 (542415)

This oak-dominated wine doesn't bang you over the head with wood. Instead, a nutty nose of almond gives way to pecans and pears on the palate of this graceful, woody Chardonnay. The fruit builds in intensity through the wine with a ripe peach finish. You can pair this lighter-bodied white with light, white meats or freshwater fish.

Thomas & Vaughan Vintners 1999 Chardonnay Vintner's Select

Niagara Peninsula VQA $13.95

Like those plush toys for children, this wine is soft and supple all over. Nice cedar-grilled pear and apple notes turn into a banana cream pie on the palate. Rich, crisp acidity keeps the backbone of the wine and helps to steer it to a soft landing. Chill and serve at a patio party.

Willow Heights Winery 1999 Chardonnay Reserve Stefanik Vineyard

Niagara Peninsula VQA $32.95 (487025)

Roasted, buttery nuts with a mild citrus backing give this single vineyard offering a complexity that makes it an ideal food-matching wine. The subtle touch of sweetness on the palate, with toasty oak and fruit sharing the stage, give it enough substance to go the distance. Serve this hardy white with smoky meat dishes or beside an aged cheese platter.

QUITE GOOD

Cave Spring Cellars 1999 Chardonnay Beamsville Bench

Niagara Peninsula VQA $12.95 (228551)

This light and simple Chardonnay offers some smoky bacon and toasted nutty notes. A touch more fruit on the palate gives the oak some balance with a lemon profile that seems to come alive on the finish. Built for those quick meals during the week.

Creekside Estates 1999 Chardonnay

Niagara Peninsula VQA $13.95

A mix of toast, vanilla and pear notes offers an attractive entry to this light-bodied offering. A lightly oaked touch on the palate with a soft finish makes this wine a match with seafood or fresh-water fish.

Daniel Lenko Estate Winery 1999 Old Vines Chardonnay

Niagara Peninsula VQA $19.95

This Chardonnay has a one-track mind. Fruit, fruit and more fruit makes for an expressive, groovy and splashy wine. It will take your senses on a wild, fruity ride. Great party wine.

Harbour Estates Winery 1999 Chardonnay Reserve

Niagara Peninsula VQA $22.95

Lush tropical fruit notes of pear and passion fruit lead into a load of fruit on the palate. The expressive fruit is attractive, but a sweet touch on the palate makes it a sipper rather than a dinner wine.

Henry of Pelham Family Estate Winery 1999 Chardonnay Reserve

Niagara Peninsula VQA $13.95 (252833)

A subtle Chardonnay that expresses lemon and grapefruit on the nose with a little oak added to the palate. It's drinking well now, so pair it with white meat dishes or salads.

Hillebrand Estates Collectors' Choice 1998 Chardonnay Barrel Aged

Niagara Peninsula VQA $15.95 (291682)

This light and airy Chardonnay leans on the fruit for its complexity. Citrus and melon notes carry over to the palate. A subtle touch of vanilla gives the wine some depth. Rounds out with a slightly sweet finish.

Lakeview Cellars 1999 Chardonnay Beamsville Bench

Niagara Peninsula VQA $9.95 (307165)

On the nose lots of fragrant candied fruit such as apples and melons. The fruit carries the load from beginning to end for this light-bodied Chardonnay. A slightly hot finish gives it a little kick in the pants. Could kick through some Chinese takeout.

Magnotta Winery 1999 Chardonnay Barrel Fermented

Niagara Peninsula VQA $14.95

A light, lean offering with an interesting note of cinnamon behind the pear and apple highlights. A streak of acidity keeps the wine alive and makes it a good match for spicy dishes.

Maleta Vineyards 1999 Chardonnay Reserve

Niagara Peninsula VQA $18.95

Supple notes of apricot, pear and peach mingle with some roasted nuts. The fruit carries the wine through to the finish. A soft, fruity Chardonnay with enough body to make it a mid-week sipper.

Malivoire Wine Co. 1999 Chardonnay
Niagara Peninsula VQA $21.95 (573147)
A soft Chardonnay with ripe pears and apples wrapped inside a blanket of oak. A light wash of fruit coats the palate, and the oak loosens its grip toward the finish. A wine to kick back and relax with.

Marynissen Estates 1999 Chardonnay Barrel Fermented 'F' Marynissen Vineyard
Niagara Peninsula VQA $13.50 (391037)
Picture a pear and a banana hanging out in a sauna. Cedar, toast and tropical fruit are the dominant characteristics of this wine. It's resting on the lean side, so pair this one with light dishes.

Mission Hill Estate Winery 1999 Cordillera Okanagan Chardonnay Anarchist Mountain
Okanagan Valley VQA $11.95 (574103)
Anarchist is the right tag for this wine. Comes across as a Sauvignon Blanc with lemon grassy fingerprints all over it. Although not even close to a Chardonnay, it's damn good, with a great lingering finish. One rebel without a cause.

Peller Estates 1998 Private Reserve Chardonnay Barrel Aged
Niagara Peninsula VQA $25 (981266)
With its lemon grass and floral notes, this one has an interesting profile for a Chardonnay. Although barrel-aged, the wine focuses on the fruit with lemon and banana on the palate. A slight vanilla thread finds its way through, making itself known on the finish. There's a sweet hint in the wine that gives it an added complexity. This would go well with a good book.

Southbrook Winery 1998 Chardonnay Triomphe

Niagara Peninsula VQA $17.95 (533315)
The bouquet points to a big, old Chardonnay with wafts of vanilla, banana and pears. Yet it stalls slightly on the palate as it shows a lighter side with more subtle fruit flavours. There's a bit of spice on the finish, which gives the wine an added boost.

Southbrook Winery 1999 Chardonnay Triomphe

Niagara Peninsula VQA $19.95 (533315)
A split-personality wine with a lot of oak on the nose and tropical fruit on the palate. Although not fully integrated, the wine has enough heft to carry it through a meat lover's meal.

Stoney Ridge Estate Cellars 1998 Reserve Chardonnay

Niagara Peninsula VQA $16 (280818)
A tropical fruit cocktail with big banana, peach, pear and honeydew melon flavours all over the wine. From the first sniff through to the finish, the fruit dominates. This is a big, juicy Chardonnay that would be perfect for the cocktail hour.

Stoney Ridge Estate Cellars 1999 Chardonnay Bench

Niagara Peninsula VQA $11.95 (293829)
A tropical fruit splash with ripe peaches, mango and passion fruit. The fruity flavours wash over the entire wine from start to finish. This would be an ideal wine as a pre-dinner cocktail.

Strewn Wines 1998 Terroir Chardonnay Strewn Vineyard

Niagara Peninsula VQA $12.45 (542415)

Although the bouquet is dominated by oak, the palate offers a more integrated profile for a Chardonnay. The oak gives way to some light flavours of banana and butterscotch. The oak tends to fight with the fruit, but the good weight of the wine indicates that a few more months in the bottle and the wine should be ready for some fancy dining.

Sumac Ridge Estate Winery 1998 Chardonnay

Okanagan Valley VQA $12.75 (125583)

If you're looking for a wine to appeal to a wide range of palates, this one could do the trick. Full of fruity apple and banana flavours, there's a sweet touch on the palate that accents the fruit. The finish has a slightly candied flavour. Lightly oaked with loads of fruit, it's definitely a crowd-pleaser.

Sumac Ridge Estate Winery 1999 Chardonnay Private Reserve

Okanagan Valley VQA $15.95 (393710)

This simple Chardonnay focuses on the fruit. A little oak on the palate gives the wine some body. A streak of acidity controls the fruit and a slightly hot finish makes it a good match for B.C. salmon.

Thirteenth Street Winery 1999 Sandstone Chardonnay Barrel Fermented

Niagara Peninsula VQA $21.95

It's as if a woodsman took a chainsaw and cut down a forest. Huge oak notes prevail with a hint of petrol on the nose. Trees continue to fall on the palate with fruit way behind. The panel was split on this gigantic Chardonnay. It has potential to age very well as the oak subsides, but if you're really into oak, drink it now. Big, gamey meats would be the best match for this monster.

GEWÜRZTRAMINER

Can you say Gewürztraminer? If you can, and you aren't afraid to ask for it by name in a restaurant, pat yourself on the back. You're in the minority. Gewürztraminer (pronounced Ga-vertz-trau-mee-ner) is a highly aromatic white wine with an unfriendly consumer label. Encumbered by that multisyllabic German handle (Tramin is the town in which the grape was discovered and "gewurz" means spiced or perfumed), Gewürztraminer has fought an uphill public relations battle ever since.

Known around the *Vines* office as the G-wine —simple because it's easier to say—Gewürztraminer is on the rise in Canada. Growers can tell when it's ready to harvest by its pink skin and know that the journey toward a fine Gewürztraminer starts with acid levels. The grapes require a cooler growing season to reach the higher acidity levels that establish the foundation of a well-made G-wine, so, not surprisingly, the little grape that could appears to have found an ideal home in B.C. and Ontario.

With acid levels in check, it becomes a winemaker's task to extract the grape's true potential. A hallmark G-wine will be a deeply golden colour and will have a very perfumed nose with loads of ripe lychee fruit and soapy, rosewater characteristics. Ripe tropical fruits can also make an appearance. Other notable characteristics include a full body with a higher alcohol range than most whites. Also look for a slight copper tinge.

Alsace is the best place to start when looking for a benchmark Gewürztraminer. The Alsatians pioneered the varietal and have consistently produced beautiful Gewürztraminers. In Canada, the potential is definitely there. Winemakers in both British Columbia and Ontario have hit the target—but not consistently. Once consistency has been established, Canada will become known for its delicious Gewürztraminer. Multiculturalism at it best.

—AA, LB, GP, WS, CW

HIGHLY RECOMMENDED

Daniel Lenko Estate Winery 1999 Gewürztraminer

Niagara Peninsula VQA $15.95

Head of the G-wine class. For the second year in a row, Daniel Lenko's Gewürztraminer has been highly favoured by the *Vines* panel. It has all the trappings of a classic G-wine. It excels aromatically with ripe lychee fruit and a touch of rosewater in behind. The ripe fruit carries forth with lychee holding the torch. It completes the cycle with a smooth finish and a slight kick. Although best of the pack, a touch more acidity would have vaulted this wine into the *Vines* Award category.

Tinhorn Creek Vineyards 2000 Gewürztraminer

Okanagan Valley VQA $12.95 (530675)

When you think of Marilyn Monroe, what goes through you mind? Sexy, luscious, full-bodied, sweet, alluring, frisky and youthful would be good adjectives. Now, this G-wine from Tinhorn captures the essence of Blondie in a bottle. Its luscious scents of lychee, pink grapefruit and honeydew melon are quite captivating. A touch of sweetness caresses the tropical fruits and takes them home for a nice, lingering finish. A bit racy, this medium-bodied white is quite alluring on its own or with *Some Like It Hot*.

RECOMMENDED

Calona Vineyards Artist Series 1999 Gewürztraminer

Okanagan Valley VQA $11.95 (237453)

Thoughts of fashionably thin women modelling fancy perfumes enter the mind. Perfumed aromas of lemons and limes mingle with a touch of rose-scented soap. A subtle sweetness on the palate enhances the tropical fruits. Light and airy on the finish, much like those models. Best enjoyed while mingling.

Daniel Lenko Estate Winery 2000 Gewürztraminer

Niagara Peninsula VQA $15.95

The 2000 vintage is similar to the '99 version with all the typical lychee fruit and rosewater notes. A touch of sweetness follows to the finish. Still finding its legs during the panel tasting, this one should open up to be a wonderfully aromatic and balanced G-wine.

Hernder Estate Wines 2000 Gewürztraminer
Niagara Peninsula VQA $11.95 (515411)
If you've ever taken a lemon balm leaf and rubbed it between your fingers, you'd know the aroma of this wine. The lemony, leafy characteristics carry over to the palate. An interesting, light and lean G-wine with a slight oily finish. A great match for oysters and shrimp.

Jackson-Triggs 1999 Proprietors' Reserve Gewürztraminer
Okanagan Valley VQA $12.95 (543843)
For one taster, sipping this wine conjured up the image of a lemon-scented bubble bath and a pillow of rose petals. Diluted lemon with a dash of rosewater carries this wine through the palate with an interesting touch of anise. Refreshingly clean and crisp, the wine would be a great partner to a pork roast or, served chilled, for just sipping with a partner.

Konzelmann Estate Winery 1999 Gewürztraminer Late Harvest (0)
Niagara Peninsula VQA $13.95 (392357)
This one captures the aroma of dried rose petals. A deep, rich, golden colour points to an extended contact with the skins, which shows in the intensity of the flavours. A sweet touch adds to the attractive ripe fruit and rounds out the finish. Made for those long weekends by the lake or watching dusk take over the sky.

Quails' Gate Estate Winery 2000 Gewürztraminer
Okanagan Valley VQA $15.95 (585745)
Spice is nice. Hints of ripe lychee notes with a touch of sweet spice sum up the essence of this well-made wine. Dashes of spice and fruit unfold on the palate; the finish is subtle, crisp and hot. Perfect for a stir-fry.

Sumac Ridge Estate Winery 1999 Gewürztraminer Private Reserve
Okanagan Valley VQA $13.95 (142893)
Eau de Gewürztraminer is the latest fragrance for both men and women. Subtle hints of rose petals and sweet lemons have fused to create a new fragrance that is taking Europe by storm. A touch of sweetness leads to a tart ending. One drop behind the ears and you won't be going home alone. A great food companion.

Vineland Estates Winery 1999 Gewürztraminer Reserve Frontier Vineyard
Niagara Peninsula VQA $22 (563353)
Subtle aromas with ever-so-light dashes of rose-water and lemon. But once in the mouth, lemon oil and lychee nut flavours crash down. This finely balanced, clean and light offering would be best paired with something spicy—spicy food that is.

Wild Goose Vineyards 2000 Gewürztraminer
Okanagan Valley VQA $12.95 (414748)
One taster had a memory of standing under a linden tree in full blossom during a spring rain. Essences of lemons and tea leaves predominate. Soft and supple, the wine leaves a lingering finish. Memories for a rainy day.

QUITE GOOD

Cave Spring Cellars 1999 Gewürztraminer Estate Bottled
Niagara Peninsula VQA $14.95 (302059)
This one was a little shy and really didn't begin to dance until it hit the palate. Delicate rose and lemon made it interesting. This wine was built to dance with food.

CedarCreek Estate Winery 2000 Gewürztraminer

Okanagan Valley VQA $13.95 (240978)
Lemon meringue pie in a bottle. All lemon with a touch of cream-filling sweetness. It had the markings of a fine wine but lost its way home.

Creekside Estate Winery 2000 Gewürztraminer

Niagara Peninsula VQA $12.95 (593640)
A lightweight contender in the G-wine category. Candied lemon drops carried the card, but it was a little out of shape for the match. It could hold its ground if paired with lighter dishes—or even soup.

Hawthorne Mountain Vineyards 2000 Gewürztraminer

Okanagan Valley VQA $12.95 (593640)
This wine could easily be mistaken for a Sauvignon Blanc. We even had to check to see if the wrong bottle had been poured. Fresh-cut grass, gooseberry and lemon balm aromas caught the panel off guard. The lemon dominated the palate with a nice balance on the finish. A well-made white—but we couldn't find the G in this one.

Henry of Pelham Family Estate Winery 1999 Gewürztraminer

Niagara Peninsula VQA $13.95 (268359)
Light and airy with pink grapefruit and lemons on the nose. Concentrated acidity leaves this wine best suited for lean meats and stews. A touch too tart, but with the right dish, this wine would be right at home.

Hillebrand Estates 2000 Gewürztraminer Vineyard Select
Niagara Peninsula VQA $9.95 (291740)
If you're looking for a quick G-wine fix until the store restocks the shelves, grab this one. Typical rosewater and bits of lemon carry through this light, lean and affordable wine. Hint—best enjoyed chilled in an open field listening to some fine jazz.

Konzelmann Estate Winery 1999 Gewürztraminer Late Harvest (2)
Niagara Peninsula VQA $13.95 (200550)
All the elements of a typical Gewürztraminer with some ripe lychee fruit dominating. A subtle sweetness on the palate continues the trend, but as the acidity kicks in, a touch too much alcohol appears on the back nine. A fine offering for enjoying on the back patio.

Larch Hills Winery 1999 Gewürztraminer
Salmon Arm, B.C. $12.50 (708875)
Interesting lime-peel notes wash over this wine. Hints of typical Gewürztraminer appear on the palate, although an overpowering acidity takes this one home quickly. The wine is ideal for cutting through hot and spicy dishes.

Malivoire Wine Co. 2000 Gewürztraminer Moira Vineyard
Niagara Peninsula VQA $24.95 (542422)
A G-wine in the body of a Sauvignon Blanc would be a perfect description. Intense lemon and grass notes dominate. The grassy flavours take over on the palate, and there's a hint of mineral at the base. Lacks the classic characteristics of Gewürztraminer, but it is still a wonderful wine.

Peller Estates 2000 Gewürztraminer Vineyard Series

Niagara Peninsula VQA $13.95 (981340)

The Martha Stewart of the G-wines. Simple with a touch of style. Hints of rosewater with a sprinkle of sweetness on the palate. Serve in a designer ice bucket.

Reif Estate Winery 2000 Gewürztraminer

Niagara Peninsula VQA $12.30 (127985)

Mr. Tangerine Man was all over this one from start to finish. If you're a fan of the tangerine—give this Gewürztraminer a taste. A touch of sweetness is followed closely with a sharp hit on the finish. Hot and tasty—you can't get this in the produce section.

Strewn Wines 1999 Gewürztraminer

Niagara Peninsula VQA $13.75 (576017)

An interesting take on Gewürztraminer. In a blind-fold tasting of this wine, it would be very difficult to select it as a Gewurztraminer. With pineapple and mango on the nose, you'd be at a loss for clues. On the palate, the fruit duo continues to hide any trace of classic G-wine flavours. Although not typical of a G-wine, it's well constructed with a medium build and a lingering finish.

Vineland Estates Winery 1999 Gewürztraminer

Niagara Peninsula VQA $12.95 (434779)

A light G-wine all the way around. Subtle fragrant nose with a slightly tart touch on the palate. Serve with a lightly dressed tossed salad.

PINOT BLANC

If Pinot Gris is a distant cousin of Pinot Noir, then Pinot Blanc is its long-lost cousin. Considered a mutant of the Pinot Noir family, it is so far removed from the grape's family tree that it was adopted by the Chardonnay family for many years and called Pinot Chardonnay.

This is another fringe varietal not widely produced on the world stage, and some Canadian wineries have taken a turn at trying to make Pinot Blanc a wine favourite. Winemakers favour this grape because of its habit of early ripening as well as its vigorous and productive capabilities. Although not overtly aromatic, its frequently high acidity and full body allow many producers to design the wine to be consumed with food. Again, as with Pinot Gris, there is no real benchmark for winemakers to aim for.

—AA, PB, SS, WS, CW

FOOD PAIRING SUGGESTIONS
It depends on the winemaking style. Unoaked Pinot Blanc can be paired with spicy dishes such as Asian cuisine, grilled vegetables or steamed shellfish. Oaked offerings go well with smoked fish and other lean meats.

HIGHLY RECOMMENDED

Jackson-Triggs 1999 Proprietors' Reserve Pinot Blanc

Okanagan Valley VQA $11.95 (543827)

Have you ever been to a peach-canning factory? Close your eyes, unleash this one and voilà, you're there. One swirl of the glass and peaches and apricots dance off the rim. The peach notes carry nicely into the palate with a slightly sweet touch. The attractive mouth-feel will quickly dispel Pinot Blanc's stature as a second-class citizen to Chardonnay. A perfect match with one of those oversized lounge chairs or to complement a spicy dish.

RECOMMENDED

Calona Vineyards Copper Moon Harvest 1999 Pinot Blanc

Okanagan Valley VQA $11.95 (578526)

This is what Five Alive would be like if you added a touch of spirit. Uncork Copper Moon for some lemon, lime and other citrus flavours, which make this a wonderful brunch wine candidate. A rather dry white with a long finish, the zesty fruit flavours would pair nicely with mussels, oysters or fish in a light lemon sauce.

Calona Vineyards Sandhill 2000 Pinot Blanc Burrowing Owl Vineyard

Okanagan Valley VQA $14.95 (541185)

A delicate toasty note opens this well-made wine, which delivers primarily citrus characteristics on the palate. Deft oak aging helps round out the mouth-feel and extend the lingering finish without muting the expressive fruit flavours. A crisp, attractive wine with assertive persistence. This is food-friendly and stylish.

Inniskillin Okanagan Winery 1999 Pinot Blanc

Okanagan Valley VQA $12.95 (522748)

Smoked salmon should watch out for this Pinot Blanc; it has finally met its match. Melon, apple and some toasty notes point toward a delicious wine made for cleansing the palate after some smoked salmon. Just be sure to tell the salmon it was warned.

Mission Hill Estate Winery 2000 Pinot Blanc

Okanagan Valley VQA $12.95 (300301)

This is one zestfully, clean and crisp Pinot Blanc. Big, hefty notes of tropical fruit like pineapple, lemons and banana dominate the bouquet. On the palate, the lush tropical fruit salad continues to dominate the wine. It's balanced by a streak of acidity that keeps the wine lively and full of vigour. Best enjoyed while mingling.

Strewn Wines 1999 Pinot Blanc

Niagara Peninsula VQA $12.50 (522748)

It's like cutting the lawn under a lemon tree with a bit of bark thrown in. The aromas were neutral at first, but this wine proved to be a late bloomer. Oak aging adds layers of vanilla and cedar flavours, but without the clean lemon notes it would be nothing. This is certainly not a big wine, but it is elegant and made with a deft touch.

QUITE GOOD

Calona Vineyards Artist Series 1999 Pinot Blanc

Okanagan Valley VQA $10.95 (261024)

Like that classic rock song brags, it's here for a good time, not a long time. It starts out with a burst of banana, pears and mango. As it moves forward, it loses a bit of energy—sort of like Charles Oakley in the fourth quarter. Great for a large party or half-time refreshment.

Hester Creek Estate Winery 1998 Signature Release Barrel Fermented Pinot Blanc

Okanagan Valley VQA $14.95 (484485)

Smells like a Chardonnay, looks like a Chardonnay, but wait, it's not a Chardonnay! A touch too much oak, which may settle down with age, masks the fruity notes of Pinot Blanc. Built for those who like some wood with their wine. Pair with some oily fish or duck to help temper the sharp edge.

Hester Creek Estate Winery 1999 Pinot Blanc

Okanagan Valley VQA $9.85 (467316)

Felt the urge to polish some dusty furniture after getting a whiff of this one. Lemon oil with a touch of woody oak is the best description. Surprisingly, this introduction was followed with pineapple and peach on the palate. Although it comes across as a bit too neutral, it's the wine equivalent of the classic line in *The Third Man* about how little Switzerland has to show for enjoying hundreds of years of neutrality—the cuckoo clock.

Hillebrand Estates 2000 Vineyard Select Pinot Blanc

Niagara Peninsula VQA $9.25 (422402)

Think melon-flavoured Jolly Rancher. There's the temptation to write this wine off merely as cheap and cheerful, but the wonderful lingering finish, which expands in the mouth, will change your mind. Ripe fruit makes for some nice melon and tropical fruit notes, and the lemon-like acidity keeps the flavours taut. Throwing a big bash? This would be a fan favourite.

St. Hubertus Estate Winery 1999 Vintner's Reserve Pinot Blanc

Okanagan Valley VQA $10.50 (344978)

Open this aromatic white, place by the kitchen window and watch as the apple pie thieves come for the goods. A bit slippery on the palate with the apple notes carrying over. Chill and serve—invite the pie snatchers if you like.

Sumac Ridge Estate Winery 1999 Pinot Blanc

Okanagan Valley VQA $10.95 (327882)

The Ally McBeal of the tasting—a lean, light Pinot Blanc with curious charms. An overabundance of citrus notes on the palate leads to an acidic wine, but the flavours that linger are less zesty and slightly twisted. This is simple, straightforward wine that's all about fun. Food is a must, which possibly is where the Ally McBeal comparisons begin and end.

Vineland Estates Winery 2000 Pinot Blanc

Niagara Peninsula VQA $14.95 (563478)

An expressive young wine, this will develop to be a pleasant blend of ripe lemon, melon and creamy butter flavours. Fragrant and spicy on the nose, this is tasty and fairly assertive on the palate. A classic taste of fresh, mouth-watering fruit, vanilla and spice.

Wild Goose Vineyards 2000 Pinot Blanc

Okanagan Valley VQA $11.95 (414722)

Go to the market and buy some ripe honeydew melon and lemons. Cut up the melon, add some lemon peel, throw it in a blender and mix. If you could drink this, it would taste a lot like Wild Goose's 2000 offering. Good mouth-feel with melons dominating the palate. The slightly high acidity makes it a perfect food matcher.

PINOT GRIS

For many wine lovers, Pinot Gris is like the cousin you've always heard the family talk about but never got the chance to meet. You know, Cousin Larry, a successful something-or-other who lives in a town far away. You get the odd Christmas card from him, but that's about it.

In fact, Pinot Gris just happens to be a distant cousin of the popular Pinot Noir grape family. Thus the name Pinot Gris, with its greyish blue or brownish pink skin. And if the Pinot Gris happens to reside in Italy or is made by an Italian-born producer, it becomes Pinot Grigio.

In terms of style, Pinot Gris can be made light and spritzy (usually the Pinot Grigio side of the fence) or rich and oily (hello, card-carrying Pinot Gris) depending on the winemaker and vintage. Neither style is overtly aromatic and, when looking for a well-made Pinot Gris, the levels of extract and acidity are what can make or break this wine.

FOOD PAIRING SUGGESTIONS
Fish (both fresh and saltwater), oysters and other shellfish. Pinot Gris' acidity level makes it a matchmaker with spicy foods—think Indian, Asian and Middle Eastern cuisine.

In Canada, Pinot Gris is the new kid on the block that everyone wants to play with. This year's panel had a number of debut vintages to assess among a slate of wines that featured a vast number of winemaking styles. Some were aged with oak and refined by malolactic fermentation. Most were produced in stainless steel fermentation, but often without a focused style. With the varying styles came some great and some not-so-great successes. There's a lot of potential for Pinot Gris in both British Columbia and Ontario, but winemakers need to refine their approach.
—AA, PB, SS, WS, CW

VINES AWARD

The following two Pinot Gris registered the same marks in each category. Even after a blind taste-off between the two, it was decided that both wines were worthy of a *Vines* Award. We felt that each exhibited the markings of a benchmark Pinot Gris. Both wines set the standards that others may follow in years to come as the wine gains popularity in Canada.

Burrowing Owl Estate Winery 2000 Pinot Gris
Okanagan Valley VQA $20 (510951)
Have you ever popped a tropical fruit candy into your mouth and suddenly had your mouth water uncontrollably? This wine turns on those same taste bud taps. Subtle notes of lemon and lime aroma give way to mouth-filling pineapple flavours mingled with lemon and lime on the palate. There's also a touch of sweetness on the palate with a clean, crisp finish. A wonderful expression of Pinot Gris, the mouth-watering fruit makes a wonderful complement to spicy and flavourful foods like sausage and Chinese food, but it's also full-flavoured enough to serve on its own.

Malivoire Wine Co. 2000 Pinot Gris

Niagara Peninsula VQA $17.95 (591305)
Think pink. Pink grapefruit flavours thread through
this hallmark Pinot Gris. The wine exhibits the
pinkish hue you should expect to see in quality
Pinot Gris. Contact with the grape skins gives
the wine a subtle colouring and adds some
complexity to the wine's flavour and volume to
its mouth-feel. Grapefruit and lemon grass leap
from the glass and carry over to the palate. A
complex and classy white that would go well
with Asian fusion cuisine or on the porch during
a spring shower.

HIGHLY RECOMMENDED

Mission Hill Estate Winery Reserve 1999 Pinot Gris

Okanagan Valley VQA $15.95 (537076)
The sweet smell of ripe Georgia peaches and a
touch of almonds add a dash of complexity to
this fresh, clean and peachy wine. Nice lingering
finish rounds it out. Ideal for a simple gathering or
a quiet night in.

Vineland Estates Winery 2000 Pinot Gris

Niagara Peninsula VQA $16.95 (563460)
This is for those who savour the aromas of
lemon tea. The follow-up to last year's *Vines*
Award winning vintage, Vineland's 2000 wine
showcases the winery's patented aromatic and
slightly sweet style of winemaking. This crowd-
pleasing style of Pinot Gris is delicate enough
to pair harmoniously with dinner but is rich and
flavourful, too. Pleasant by the glass or with your
favourite stir-fry.

RECOMMENDED

Gehringer Brothers Estate Winery 1999 Private Reserve Pinot Gris

Okanagan Valley VQA $14.70 (347203)

The key to the success of this wine is its acidity. With a hint of pink grapefruit on the nose, the wine opens up on the palate to unleash a very crisp, lively offering. The acidity enhances the lemon and mineral flavours and carries them through to the extended finish. This is an ideal wine for spicy Indian dishes because of its ability to cut through the spices and refresh the palate.

Hester Creek Estate Winery 1999 Pinot Gris

Okanagan Valley VQA $13.85 (560037)

Definitely a New World approach to Pinot Gris, which split the panel into two camps. Some were taken by the touch of oak aging that added complexity to the finished wine. Others thought the oak spice masked the fruit on the palate. Here's what we all could agree upon: A complex wine with intricate aromas including lots of fruit notes and nice grapefruit and lime flavours on the palate.

Inniskillin Wines 2000 Pinot Grigio

Niagara Peninsula VQA $11.95 (348979)

That's Mr. Pinot Grigio to you. Inniskillin offers up the Andy Garcia of the Pinot family. Crisp, clean and full of zesty lemon, this is a straight-to-business wine. It's focused and fresh on the palate with bright citrus notes carrying through to a slightly hot finish. This wine is in the business of pleasure.

Mission Hill Estate Winery Private Reserve 1999 Pinot Gris

Okanagan Valley VQA $12.95 (563981)

Froot Loops for the wine lover. Tangerine and mandarin orange tickle the nose. Tropical fruits with a couple of slices of peach thrown in tantalize the palate. Rich and smooth in the mouth, this B.C. wine is rounded out with a slight acidity and a clean, lingering finish. Great food matcher.

QUITE GOOD

Calona Vineyards Artist Series 1999 Pinot Gris

Okanagan Valley VQA $10.95 (505222)

Sometimes simplicity is needed to soothe the soul and the mind. This easy-drinking wine caresses the air with light lemon and apple aromas. Ripe melon with a touch of almond flavours gently cover the palate. A touch of sweetness brings this wine home. A great companion for a family picnic or quiet time with a Carol Shield's book.

Château des Charmes Estate Winery 2000 Pinot Gris

Niagara Peninsula VQA $11.95 (593749)

This one has the perfect colour of a Pinot Gris— a pleasant salmon pink. But the subdued aroma profile of light lemon points to a leaner offering. On the palate, this welterweight extends a concentrated mouth-feel, which leads to a slightly hot finish.

Harvest Estate Winery 2000 Pinot Gris
Niagara Peninsula VQA $10.95 (579995)
The perfect wine for a larger gathering like a family reunion or afternoon wedding. Subtle aromas of lemon fresh perfume, with a slightly sweet touch on the palate. Florals and fruit are featured flavours on the palate. A food-friendly, value-priced offering that lacks the depth to serve as an aperitif. However, it will find its stride with roast pork or chicken and grilled vegetables.

Hawthorne Mountain Vineyards 1999 Pinot Gris
Okanagan Valley VQA $16.95 (704999)
This one would appeal to the folks who enjoy oak. At first, a dollop of oak coats the lemon aromas, but after a bit of fresh air the wine opens up and the citrus notes come crashing out of the forest. The oak points to the creamy, buttery flavours on the palate with the lemons and limes pushing forward as it sits in the glass. This is a wine made to pair with oysters and other shellfish.

Magnotta Winery 1999 Pinot Gris
Niagara Peninsula VQA $7.95
A straightforward, zesty style of Pinot Gris, Magnotta's wine features an attractive floral nose. High acids dominate the expressive apple characteristics on the palate. The zingy, crispness makes it a dinnertime wine. It needs the flavours of food to help mellow the wine's intensity.

Thomas & Vaughan Vintners 2000 Pinot Gris
Niagara Peninsula VQA $13.95
This wine's aromas conjure up images of pears and bananas—like a tropical fruit punch. The fruit turns soft and flabby on the palate. The wine would have scored higher with our panel if there had been a bit more acidity to balance out those delicious ripe fruit flavours.

RIESLING

Pity poor Riesling. The world's noble white wine grape seems destined to live forever in the shadow of easy-to-drink, easy-to-pronounce Chardonnay. The pride of Germany, Riesling is an agreeable drink that's all about the balance of fruit and acidity in the finished wine.

Unlike the prima donna Chardonnay, there's no performance-enhancing oak aging, no special additional fermentation to soften the wine or mellow its expressive flavours. Riesling is down-to-earth, a low-maintenance kind of wine. What you see in the grape is what you get in the glass.

Transplanted in any wine region of the world, it will reflect the unique soil and microclimate of the site, yet it remains unequivocally Riesling. Its identity is bulletproof. In Canada, it performs exceptionally well, and winemakers are able to consistently produce wines that range from bone-dry to opulent and sweet. We're interested

FOOD PAIRING SUGGESTIONS
Dry Rieslings are the most versatile white whites on the market for matching with cuisines as diverse as Thai, French, Mexican and Californian fusion. Also go well with freshwater and saltwater fish. Off-dry styles are excellent sipping or aperitif wines.

in drier styles here; the sweeter dessert wines are featured later in the book.

A highly aromatic wine, which offers predominantly citrus, lime and floral notes in British Columbia or Ontario vintages, Riesling will develop more of a characteristic kerosene/petrol note as it ages. While Riesling has the capacity to cellar for a long time, most consumers enjoy the young fruit characteristics of the wine as opposed to its aged grease-monkey notes.

For consumers, the upside to Riesling's second-class-citizen status means savvy wine shoppers have their pick of value-priced wines. On a value-for-money axis, it doesn't get any better than undervalued Rieslings, which generally retail in the $8–$12 range.

—AA, LB, RD, AP, GP, CW

HIGHLY RECOMMENDED

Cave Spring Cellars 2000 Off-Dry Riesling
Niagara Peninsula VQA $11.25 (234583)
Don't like Riesling? Cave Spring unleashes a triple-threat Riesling with elegant fruit aromas, great flavours and a big, balanced racy finish that'll change your mind. A most agreeable drink—open a bottle to sip, quaff with friends or to accompany a good book. The hint of sweetness makes this a crowd-pleasing style that will wow even the most unrepentant Chardonnay stick-in-the-mud.

Peller Estates 2000 Dry Riesling Private Reserve
Niagara Peninsula VQA $14.95 (981290)
Peller's dry white would feel right at home in a picnic basket. Its peach and floral aromas are more in line with a romantic nosh in the shade for two than, say, the annual company barbecue. But an outgoing wine like Peller is too classy to discriminate, even if there are sack races going on. It's the life of any party.

RECOMMENDED

Cave Spring Cellars 1999 Riesling Reserve

Niagara Peninsula VQA $14.95 (286377)

One of Orson Welles' greatest movie roles was as Harry Lime in *The Third Man*, a black marketer living in postwar Vienna. This powerful wine has a lot in common with that classic black-and-white thriller. Lime, for starters. Big-time lime aromas and flavours dominate. Plus, this well-crafted wine is a thrilling drink with a lingering finish that is as cerebral and enjoyable as one of Hollywood's greatest films.

Cave Spring Cellars 2000 Dry Riesling

Niagara Peninsula $11.25 (233635)

Don't let the dry reference scare you away. Like homemade lemonade, this delicious wine is not too tart, not too sweet. Alcohol doesn't play a principal role nor is dryness the be-all and end-all. This is an elegant wine made for the dinner table or weekends at the cottage.

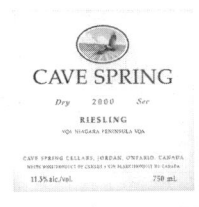

CedarCreek Estate Winery 2000 Dry Riesling

Okanagan Valley VQA $12.95 (217166)

Here's a delicate Riesling that's perfect to take fly fishing. A river of mouth-watering acidity runs through it, making it the perfect partner for the catch of the day. The same way that squeezing lemon on fish helps refresh its flavour, this crisp wine will help perk up the flavours in your finny entrées.

Daniel Lenko Estate Winery 2000 Riesling Reserve

Niagara Peninsula VQA $12.95

The 2000 vintage in Ontario and British Columbia is showing great promise for quality Rieslings. Take this fine, young example: it's subtle enough to match with your favourite steamed seafood or grilled white meat, but also well-rounded enough to be able to linger around the table afterwards with the grown-ups to gossip and talk politics.

Henry of Pelham Family Estate Winery 2000 Dry Riesling

Niagara Peninsula VQA $10.95 (268375)

It's like there's a party in the mouth and every-one's invited! The wine equivalent of Lemon Zinger tea, this Niagara Riesling has hallmark lemon/lime aromas and flavours that will wake up your taste buds.

Hernder Estate Wines 1999 Riesling Reserve

Niagara Peninsula VQA $13.95 (554238)

Anyone who has ever seen the wine aroma wheel, which breaks down the various scents commonly found in wine into easily identifiable categories, has laughed out loud on reading "wet dog." Hernder's Reserve Riesling will show you how a wine can smell like a funky animal yet still be absolutely enjoyable. There's more to this than the stench of a sopping wet Snoopy. How about ripe peaches and spring flowers and a rich core of fruit flavours that's undeniable? One sip and any guffaws will be silenced with a bright, beaming smile.

Hillebrand Estates Winery 2000
Trius Riesling Dry

Niagara Peninsula VQA $14.95 (303792)
The outlandish fashion plates on the *Absolutely Fabulous* comedy series would lap up this stylish wine. "Sweetie, darling, sweetie, this is beyond yummy—pour me another glass." It's sophisticated enough to pair with oysters and other swanky fare, but also common enough to pair with a night watching trashy television.

Quails' Gate Estate Winery 1999 Dry Riesling

Okanagan Valley VQA $11.95 (308312)
Imagine driving an old tractor through an orange grove that's overdue for harvesting and you'll conjure up some of the expressive flavours and aromas of this fine wine. Gasoline and sweet citrus notes dominate. A high degree of alcohol makes for a slightly warm finish.

Strewn Wines 1999 Riesling
Terroir Strewn Vineyard

Niagara Peninsula VQA $13.50 (467613)
Intense aromas of citrus oil and roses are featured in this focused, single-vineyard Riesling that's dry but not austere. Concentrated flavours (especially floral rose petals and tangerine peel) as well as a crisp acidity are well matched in this finely balanced wine.

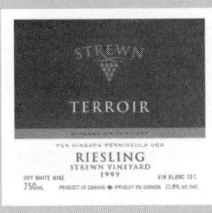

Thirty Bench Wines 1999 Riesling
Limited Yield Semi Dry

Niagara Peninsula VQA $19.95
It's hard not to like this rich and powerful wine with its wonderful combination of ripe fruit, floral aromas and firm structure. Peaches and a honeyed sweetness stand out. Lush and slightly oily on the palate, it's drinking nicely now but could be stored for three to four years.

Vineland Estates Winery 1999 Riesling Reserve

Niagara Peninsula VQA $24 (316307)

An elegant wine with the whiff and taste of citrus and a great lemony middle and finish, Vineland Estates' Reserve vintage offers mouth-filling flavours that are rounded out by a crisp and refreshing acidity.

Wild Goose Vineyards 2000 Riesling

Okanagan Valley VQA $11.95 (414730)

Bold Canadian Riesling can be as serious as Mel Gibson doing *Hamlet* or as frivolous as David Letterman's Top 10 List. This candied wine falls somewhere in between. A little bit scandalous (bright acidity and lingering rose scents), a little bit goofy (sweet palate and candied fruit flavours). A light refreshing luncheon wine that's perfect on a hot day.

QUITE GOOD

Calona Vineyards Artist Series 1999 Riesling

Okanagan Valley VQA $9.95 (237446)

Sweet spicy fruit and a luscious mouth-feel make for an uncomplicated wine best enjoyed while kicking back and hanging out with good friends. A natural selection to have on ice for your next backyard barbecue or movie night.

Cilento Wines 2000 Riesling Reserve

Niagara Peninsula VQA $11.45 (510362)

Like reading a mystery only to find the page that reveals the identity of the killer ripped out, this wine stops short in a most disappointing fashion. Its expressive citrus and floral aromas and pink grapefruit flavours are solid, but there's no big payoff.

Creekside Estates Winery 2000 Riesling
Niagara Peninsula VQA $11.95 (572446)
A gawky young wine with an abundance of acidity, this has the potential to mellow and develop into something graceful and polished. Currently, it's very tart and dry, too racy for most Riesling fans. But the lovely soft peach, apricot and lime aromas and flavours will become more unified and dominant given a couple of years of bottle age.

Daniel Lenko Estate Winery 1999 Riesling
Niagara Peninsula VQA $12.95
Fresh, soft fruit aromas and sweet palate are the best traits of this rich and enjoyable wine. Some funky petrol flavours interfere with the appealing peach and nectarine essences.

Harbour Estates Winery 1999 Riesling
Niagara Peninsula VQA $10.95
The Peach Pit was where the gang on *Beverly Hills 90210* hung out and whined. Like the twentysomething actors who played teenaged Dylan, David and Donna, Harbour Estates' wine is showing signs of premature aging. Pronounced petrol and peach pit aromas are prominent, but the sweet fruit flavours and floral notes continue to delight.

Henry of Pelham Family Estate Winery 1999 Riesling Reserve
Niagara Peninsula VQA $12.95 (283291)
Delicate rose-petal fragrance and subtle peach/apricot flavours are featured in this wallflower Riesling. Shy and subdued, it's anything but assertive, yet the underlying fruit and sharp acidity will command your attention and respect.

Henry of Pelham Family Estate Winery 1999 Off-Dry Riesling

Niagara Peninsula VQA $12.95 (557165)

Similar to Henry of Pelham's Reserve, this is another shy and delicate wine, with a hint of sweetness and searing acidity at the finish. The folks at Dale Carnegie's *How to Win Friends and Influence People* courses will tell you to speak softly so you command your listener's attention. There's probably some hard-won truth in that sentiment, but wines need a bit more assertiveness to command a wine drinker's attention.

Inniskillin Wines 2000 Riesling

Niagara Peninsula VQA $9.95 (083790)

Pink grapefruit notes combine with some atypical aromas and flavours that are more Sauvignon Blanc than Riesling in this crisp, slightly tart wine. All that zesty acidity creates a wine that needs to be invited to dinner to show off its best social graces. Serve with smoked turkey, grilled fish or pork tenderloin.

Jackson-Triggs 1999 Proprietors' Reserve Riesling

Niagara Peninsula VQA $8.95 (526244)

This off-dry wine offers lots of ripe citrus flavours shot through with a crisp green apple acidity. It's a very impressive performer for the price and is recommended as a solid all-occasion white.

Konzelmann Estate Winery 1999 Riesling Late Harvest (3)

Niagara Peninsula VQA $11.25 (200827)

A fresh and lively off-dry wine with petrol and wet wood aromas. The big fruit flavours are matched with nice acidity that help focus the lingering finish.

Konzelmann Estate Winery 2000 Riesling (1)

Niagara Peninsula VQA $9.95

Ripe fruit and floral notes are the drawing cards for this appealing vintage that is slightly flabby around the middle. Sweet and flavourful enough to serve on its own, its lower acidity makes it less successful with food.

Peller Estates 1999 Riesling Semi-Dry Vineyard Series

Niagara Peninsula VQA $10.95 (981357)

An easy-drinking wine with soft, delicate, fruit aromas and nice fruit extract on the palate. This is ripe, round and ready for your next family get-together. Its pleasant sweetness will charm.

Pillitteri Estates Winery 1999 Riesling Sweet Reserve

Niagara Peninsula VQA $10.95 (349142)

This is Germanic in style with a capital G. A very fruity, very peachy wine with petrol, wet dog and citrus characteristics on the nose. Soft fruit flavours and a slightly sweet mouth-feel are appealing, but some sherry notes and a short finish put a damper on things.

St. Hubertus 2000 Riesling

Okanagan Valley VQA $10.75 (345009)

A pleasantly crisp wine with strong lemon flavours and a slight bitterness on the finish. Fans of brisk, dry whites will thrill to this zesty Riesling.

Thirteenth Street Winery 2000 G.H. Funk Vineyards Riesling

Niagara Peninsula VQA $13.95

Strong burnt-ash aromas might prove distracting to some, but this flavourful wine recovers nicely on the palate. A balanced one-two punch of crisp acidity and lingering fruit flavours, this is drinking nicely now and has the potential to develop into an intense wine given some bottle age.

Thirty Bench Wines 1999 Dry Riesling
Niagara Peninsula VQA $11.95
Big Riesling nose of petrol, citrus and some lime zest paves the way for this wine's oily, full-bodied texture. A rich and concentrated Riesling, this zesty wine lacks fruit and finishes with a tart bitterness.

Vineland Estates Winery 1999 Dry Riesling
Niagara Peninsula VQA $9.95 (167551)
A straightforward Riesling with subtle citrus notes and very high acids. The sharp acidity dominates the fruit and the finish leaves a lingering bitter note that some might find off-putting. Best suited for the dinner table.

SAUVIGNON BLANC

Wines produced from Sauvignon Blanc offer
freshness, flavour and real concentration of fruit
that is best enjoyed young. The classic white's
characteristic aggressive zestiness is one of its
charms. Age dulls that most recognizably
Sauvignon Blanc note and, in turn, dulls the
enjoyment of the wine. Call this the wine world's
equivalent of a one-hit wonder—a glorious burst
of fame than nothing but a fleeting residual
vapour trail.

Other classic varietal characteristics include
gooseberries, cut grass or other herbaceous
notes like asparagus and green peppers, figs,
green apples, grapefruit and cat pee (yes, cat
pee; don't wince). What the French refer to as
Pipi de chat (doesn't that sound so much more
elegant?) is an acceptable note for the archetypal
French Sauvignon Blanc from Sancerre and
Pouilly-Fumé. You might, however, be happy to

FOOD PAIRING SUGGESTIONS
Oysters and scallops,
funky cheese especially
Gruyère and goat's
cheese, chicken, fish and
pasta in a cream sauce.

hear that there's little tomcat stench in most fruit-forward New World examples, but they lack the aging potential of their elegant French cousins. In extremely ripe Sauvignon, the fruit notes become more tropical in nature. Papaya and passion fruit are common descriptors.

Sauvignon Blanc has been grown for centuries in France. The rest of the wine world has only caught on in the past two decades or so. New Zealand has led the charge and has become a leader in producing some of the more impressive Sauvignon Blancs in the world. Sauvignon Blanc vintages from New World wine regions are gaining popularity with consumers because of their upfront and attractive fruit characteristics. A growing number of dedicated vintners in British Columbia and Ontario are falling in step with their counterparts in New Zealand, California, Australia and South Africa.

The success of Sauvignon Blanc in Ontario and British Columbia seems assured if the wines are simply made. Oak-aged wines, which are some-times though, frustratingly, not always identified as Fumé Blanc on the label, risk losing the bright and fresh fruit, just as the lesson of subtle oak aging was learned with Chardonnay, so too will domes-tic vintners tame the two-by-four thwack of their Sauvignons. Sumac Ridge in British Columbia is leading the way with a Bordeaux-style blend that pairs Sauvignon Blanc with Sémillon.

—JB, JD, VH, RP

VINES AWARD

Peninsula Ridge Estates 2000 Sauvignon Blanc

Niagara Peninsula VQA $18.95

Talk about judging a book by its cover. The label says Sauvignon Blanc and the wine is Sauvignon Blanc from start to finish. Open the cover and aromas of gooseberry, grass, citrus, cat's pee and grapefruit greet your nose. Reading on gives you a mouthful of crisp acidity with zesty citrus and delicious tropical notes. The plot line is balanced, and the conclusion is long and lemony. This is no knock-off of Marlborough or Sancerre, but it's a classic varietal.

HIGHLY RECOMMENDED

Cilento Wines 2000 Sauvignon Blanc Reserve

Niagara Peninsula VQA $18.95 (510251)

A stylish and elegant wine that starts from the blocks with a burst of wonderful aromas (herbaceous, cat's pee, grapefruit) that sets the nose tingling. Down the straight it sets a cracking pace, with sweet and sour flavours (citrus, asparagus) matched with racy mineral acidity. The finish is a tad shorter than the rest of the performance would lead you to expect, but overall this wine really performs.

Harbour Estates Winery 2000 Sauvignon Blanc

Niagara Peninsula VQA $15.95

Typical cat's pee, grassy and mineral aromas, followed by a slightly off-dry palate with great fruit intensity that combines citrus and tropical fruits. Wonderful acids, good balance and a medium finish. Harbour Estates hints of the sea, and this would be terrific with seafood and shellfish.

Reif Estate Winery 2000 Sauvignon Blanc
Niagara Peninsula VQA $12.95

A rich, complex, aromatic nose that's rife with citrus, mineral and grassiness leads to a real mouthful of spicy, citrus and some tropical notes. With good acidity in harmonious balance with the fruit and a medium finish, this is a very well-made wine, great alone or with food. Try it with oysters.

Vineland Estates Winery 2000 Sauvignon Blanc
Niagara Peninsula VQA $11.95

All the classic aromas clamour for attention from the glass: gooseberries, grapefruit, minerals and grass, with petrol, mint and honey trying to make themselves heard. Once they've been quietened down, the wine delivers a lush mélange of citrus and soft, sweet, tropical fruit. Great mouth-feel and a long finish.

RECOMMENDED

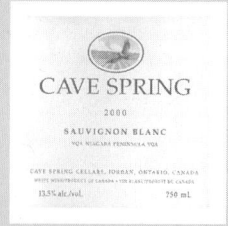

Cave Spring Cellars 2000 Sauvignon Blanc
Niagara Peninsula VQA $12.95 (529933)

Just the music you hope to hear from this varietal: notes of minerals, grassiness, cat's pee and gooseberry rise clearly from the glass as you settle in. On the palate, nicely modulated, zesty acids play harmoniously with citrus flavours. This composition is well scored, and it's a symphony of sensations you won't leave unfinished.

Creekside Estates 2000 Sauvignon Blanc
Niagara Peninsula VQA $17.95 (572206)

This is very good food wine. It has classic aromas of cat's pee, grassiness and citrus and a very intense and crisp palate of lemons and limes. The acids are really striking and are echoed on the long finish. The high acids just cry out for food, and with the right dish (like oysters or goat cheese), this will be delicious.

Mission Hill Estate Winery 1999
Private Reserve Sauvignon Blanc
Okanagan Valley VQA $12.95 (118893)
There isn't a lot of varietal typicity on the nose,
but there is no reserve in what it does give off:
lovely aromas of butter, honey and tropical fruit.
But surprise, surprise! On the palate it delivered
zippy acids filled out with generous citrus flavours.
Refreshing and crisp, this is a very easy drinker
with or without food.

Mission Hill Estate Winery 2000 Cordillera
Spotted Lake Sauvignon Blanc
Okanagan Valley VQA $10.95 (596007)
A summery basket of sweet and sour fruit here.
The nose gives off lemon, grapefruit, sweet melon
and pineapple, with some spicy notes. The
flavours echo this range and, although the fruit
is a bit subdued by the acids, the overall balance
is good. It's well made and it should be great
with food.

Mission Hill Estate Winery 2000
Sauvignon Blanc Reserve
Okanagan Valley VQA $16.95 (590349)
With a well-integrated and typical nose of
minerals, gooseberries and some cat's pee, this
wine is medium-bodied and well-balanced with
tangy citrus flavours. A medium-to-long finish,
great on its own or with food.

Quails' Gate Estate Winery 1999
Sauvignon Blanc Limited Release
Okanagan Valley VQA $15.95 (560946)
Giving off citrus, herbaceous and mineral notes
on the nose, this wine has a good balance of
zesty acidity and a range of fruit that includes
lemons and tropical produce like guavas. It's a
delicious mouthful with a medium, lemony finish.

Southbrook Winery 2000 Triomphe Sauvignon Blanc

Niagara Peninsula VQA $19.95 (593632)

Classique in many respects, this is a lovely, approachable Sauvignon Blanc that will satisfy many tastes. It has a rich, herbaceous nose with layers of minerals, nuts and figs and provides a lovely intense mouthful of citrus and fruit salad. All this topped off with good balance and a nice finish. Maybe not a heroic *triomphe*, but a *triomphe* nonetheless.

Stoney Ridge 1998 Bench Sauvignon Blanc

Niagara Peninsula VQA $16.95 (513705)

Rich, funky aromas waft out of the glass: honey, cinnamon, melon, even petrol and soy sauce. The acid and fruit are in good balance with predominant flavours of citrus and a medium finish. Tasters' reactions included, "This is a Sauvignon Blanc for Chardonnay lovers" and "unusual but likeable."

Sumac Ridge Estate Winery 2000 Black Sage Vineyard Sauvignon Blanc

Okanagan Valley VQA $15.95 (393736)

Rich tropical fruit and a hint of lemon on the nose are followed by delicious tropical fruits on the palate. This is a well balanced wine with zippy acids playing counterpoint to the fruit to produce a mouth-feel that's smooth and rounded. It finishes well with light fruit.

QUITE GOOD

Colio Estates Winery 1999 Sauvignon Blanc Barrel Aged

Lake Erie North Shore VQA $14.95 (500462)

A fairly light-bodied wine with aromas and flavours of tropical fruit, melons and peaches. It's not all that typical of Sauvignon Blanc, but it's a very pleasant wine that will go down well with or without food.

Hillebrand Estates 2000 Vineyard Select Sauvignon Blanc
Niagara Peninsula VQA $9.95 (386128)
A very pleasant medium-bodied wine. On the nose, there's a good variety of aromas like gooseberries, cat's pee, tropical fruit and minerals. Nice zingy acids meet the mouth and are followed by flavours of warm sunny fruits, lemons, honey and savoury notes like asparagus. Well balanced with a nice finish. This will please a range of tastes.

Pelee Island Winery 2000 Sauvignon Blanc
Pelee Island VQA $10.95 (511170)
This refreshing wine makes very pleasant company. It comes across a bit shy at first, with a reserved nose of minerals, citrus and straw. More verbose on the palate, though, where it speaks of tropical fruit and lemon and demonstrates an attractively acid tongue before retiring to a fairly quiet finish.

Peller Estate 1999 Private Reserve Sauvignon Blanc Barrel Aged
Niagara Peninsula VQA $14.95 (981308)
A fairly closed nose on this one with light grassy and asparagus aromas. The palate is more giving, though even there the citrus and herbaceous flavours tend to be understated. The oak is well balanced and offers a subtle layer of toastiness. This is not an exuberantly fruity or zippy wine, but if you really like it, you'll probably think it's quite elegant.

Southbrook Winery 1999 Sauvignon Blanc
Niagara Peninsula VQA $14.95 (954800)
This wine starts with a slightly musty nose that obscures the aromas of grapefruit, gooseberry and some tropical fruits. It shows better on the palate, which is crisp with nice citrus flavours and some intense acidity. The acidity carries through to the medium finish.

Thirteenth Street Winery 2000 G.H. Funk Vineyards Sauvignon Blanc
Niagara Peninsula VQA $16

This wine is fairly closed but carries hints of herbaceousness, minerals and petrol. The palate is anything but muted, however, with a zingy acid attack. The lemon and grapefruit flavours are a bit one-dimensional and understated, but one taster noted that this was "a nice mouthful."

Willow Heights Winery 2000 Sauvignon Blanc
Niagara Peninsula VQA $12.95

As many aromas as panel tasters here, with the line-up including classics like cat's pee, asparagus and smoky notes like grilled peppers, roasted peanuts and diesel. A bit more consensus on the palate, where there were tangy citrus and berry flavours. The overall impression was that this was a wine with individual appeal—a great reason to try it.

OTHER WHITE WINES

Other White Vinifera

If everyone were the same, the world would be a pretty boring place. That said, the same goes for wine. A number of wineries and grape growers in British Columbia and Ontario are experimenting with non-traditional varietals. They plant small acres of little-known vinifera vines like Viognier, Muscat, Chenin Blanc and others to see what the result will be in both quality and quantity. Sometimes the results are amazing, sometimes forgettable. Yet if it weren't for experimentation, Canada wouldn't be producing vinifera table wines, or even Icewine. It's like the German band Kraftwerk—if it weren't for their experimentation with technology, we may not have heard of bands like New Order and Nine Inch Nails. So, we feel it's our duty to review the odd wines— the ones you may not see on liquor store shelves.

But if you happen to stumble upon them on a wine tour, you can be the cool kid in the yard setting the trends for others to follow.

—LB, SGB, TK, RP, WS, CW

VINES AWARD

Daniel Lenko Estate Winery 2000 Viognier
Niagara Peninsula VQA $14.95
Speaking of Nine Inch Nails, if you're looking for an intense wine, this is the one to try. Huge notes of peach, guava and pineapple spin out on the palate. The fruit characteristics are mixed to the highest effect with a full body that could bring the house down. The intensity pulses through to the finish. No need to remix, just spin and sip through the night.

HIGHLY RECOMMENDED

Kacaba Vineyards 2000 Viognier
Niagara Peninsula VQA $12.95
Going to a masquerade ball? Take this wine. People will think it's a Chardonnay—yet only you will know it is the little-known Viognier. Ample pineapple notes would confuse even the most confident taster. The hint of spice on the palate points to a more complex wine—and the mask comes off with an intense mix of spice and tropical fruits on the finish. By the end of the night, you'll be playing spin the empty bottle with this winner.

Stonechurch Vineyards 1999 Morio Muscat

Niagara Peninsula VQA $11.95 (291542)

The Joy Division of the wine world, Stonechurch's Morio Muscat is a cult wine among wine lovers in Ontario. It has an intensely attractive nose— something like a well-made Gewürztraminer. Wafts of rose petal, lemon soap and pineapple attract wine fans like honeysuckle attracts hummingbirds. The oily texture and slightly spicy finish would help make any Thai dish or lean pork roast stand up and take a bow.

Stoney Ridge Cellars 2000 Chenin Blanc Kew Vineyard

Niagara Peninsula VQA $14.95

Chenin Blanc sounds more like a French novelist than a white wine. It opens with a waft of sweet grass and a foreshadow of French vanilla ice cream. The story unfolds as the sweet notes carry over to the palate with lemon grass taking the lead. It's well designed with a nice ending that leaves you yearning for more. Viva Chenin Blanc.

RECOMMENDED

Cilento Wines 1999 Auxerrois

Niagara Peninsula VQA $10.95 (510248)

Auxer-what? Primarily used as a blending wine in France, Cilento has taken Auxerrois and given it a bottle to call its own. You could call the grape a groupie of Chardonnay. It takes after Chard with notes of yellow delicious apple and faint pineapple. Its lower acidity makes it an easy drinking wine. With nothing to prove, this Auxerrois takes it easy and would be a great companion for tuna, salmon and shark.

St. Hubertus Estate Winery 2000 Chasselas
Okanagan Valley VQA $11.50 (436717)
This is indeed a unique white as it is primarily produced in Switzerland. St. Hubertus appears to be experimenting with the grape in Canada. If you close your eyes when tasting this wine, you'd swear it was a Sauvignon Blanc. Lemon grass and pink grapefruit notes flash to a citrus-dominated palate. Crisp, clean acidity would be the perfect match for some B.C. salmon.

Willow Heights Winery 2000 Auxerrois
Niagara Peninsula VQA $11.95 (537522)
This pleasant French vinifera has the bouquet of a basket of green apples with some grapefruit tossed for contrast. On the palate, citrus flavours are more expressive with the green apple profile lingering behind. With a finely balanced weight and a nice acidity, this white would be a welcome addition to Thai or Middle Eastern cuisine.

QUITE GOOD

Château des Charmes Estate Winery 1998 Auxerrois
Niagara Peninsula VQA $10.95 (114058)
A tropical fruit bowl of melon, pineapple and lime. It's a little flabby for the beach, but the sweet fruit on the palate would make it a perfect chilled wine just before dinner.

Peller Estates 1999 Muscat Vineyard Series
Niagara Peninsula VQA $10.95 (981373)
Highly aromatic with lemon, rosewater and a touch of melon. A sweet layer brings the lemon to the front with a quick finish. A touch of heat makes this ideal for spicy Thai and Middle Eastern dishes.

Hybrid Whites

"It's alive, it's alive," Dr. Frankenstein yelled of his monstrosity. If Dr. Frankenstein were a winemaker, he'd specialize in hybrid wines. Hybrid wines result from crossing two varietals in hopes of making a new grape. Grape growers are constantly experimenting with different varietals to make vines more adaptable to certain growing regions. Due to the cool climate of Canada's wine regions, there have been many experiments that have produced interesting wines. The best-known white hybrid in Canada is the Vidal grape. Its hardiness and thick skin make it an ideal late harvest and Icewine grape. Many of the hybrid wines reviewed by the panel are only available at the winery but are still worth checking out if you're on a wine tour.

—SGB, TK, WS, CW

HIGHLY RECOMMENDED

Thomas & Vaughan Vintners 1999 Semi-Sweet Vidal

Ontario VQA $10.95

Built for those with a sweet tooth. Characteristic honey and pear notes conjure up memories of a late-harvest Vidal. The fruit coats the palate with a slightly hot finish. A lean body with balanced acidity gives the wine a sturdy structure. Great wine for a large family gathering— think Thanksgiving.

RECOMMENDED

Blue Grouse Vineyards 1999 Bacchus
Vancouver Island $12.05 (969725)
Has Bacchus, the god of wine, been reincarnated as a grape yearning to be a Sauvignon Blanc? If so, he nailed this wine. The grape is actually a cross between Riesling and Müller-Thurgau—but with its aromas of cat's pee and gooseberry on the nose you'll swear it's a Sauvignon Blanc. The gooseberry carries over to the palate with a slightly sweet finish. This medium-bodied white would go well with fish dishes.

Domaine de Chaberton 2000 Madeleine Sylvaner
British Columbia VQA $10.45 (953000)
A wine that sounds like a character out of a Jane Austen novel. Madeleine loves perfume. She wears a fruit blend of lychee and honeysuckle. When her suitor leans in for a kiss on her shoulder, he is met with a lingering taste of honeysuckle and pear. Capture the moment by serving Madeleine with a fruit cocktail dish.

Larch Hills Winery 1999 Madeleine Angevine
British Columbia $11.50 (720755)
Another Madeleine, this time it's Angevine. This hybrid comes across as a blend of Chardonnay and Sauvignon Blanc. Pear, lemon grass and gooseberry swirl around this unique white. Although it's a little green on the palate, the acidity would make it a good wine to pair with lean chicken and pork.

QUITE GOOD

Calona Vineyards Artist Series 1999 Sovereign Opal

Okanagan Valley VQA $9.95 (364265)

It's like pulling up to a gas station somewhere in the orange belt of Florida. Orange blossoms and petrol notes make for an interesting fragrance. The fruit gets out of the car first with a touch of sweetness in the back seat. An ideal summer wine for sipping on the front porch.

Cilento Wines 1999 Renaissance Classic White Seyval Blanc

Ontario VQA $7.50 (602292)

A hardy grape that can take cooler temperatures, Seyval Blanc is a throwback to the early days of modern winemaking in Niagara. Although not many wineries are making this hybrid, there's something to be said for this lean white. Cilento's offering is citrus-driven with layers of lemon and lime taking the wine from start to finish. You could pair this wine with freshwater fish like walleye or bass.

Willow Heights Winery 1999 Seyval Blanc

Ontario VQA $8 (4087108)

This would be better than chilled lemonade. Big citrus notes ride the tide with some floral and mineral notes showing the age of the vines from which the grapes were harvested. The citrus continues the journey with a touch of acidity to bring it home. Easy to drink with or without food. Just make sure it's chilled.

White Blends

With single varietal wines all the rage with New World wine consumers, it's a wonder winemakers in Canada even produce blended wines, especially white blends. In most cases, blended whites are less expensive. They are also built for the drink-it-now wine consumer. With the exception of Sumac Ridge's Meritage White, the blends in this section are all over the wine map. As with all experiments, some are Eurekas! while others are Dohs!

—SGB, TK, WS, CW

VINES AWARD

Wild Goose Vineyards 2000 Autumn Gold
British Columbia $11.95 (414755)
This wine truly is gold. One of the main blending ingredients would have to be Gewürztraminer. Highly aromatic with dominant lychee notes, there are also hints of melons, pineapples and lemons. The fruit comes through on the palate, but a layer of acidity gives the wine some texture and holds off the wine's sweeter side. If you had to describe this wine in one word, it would be *luscious*. Best enjoyed on its own.

HIGHLY RECOMMENDED

Calona Vineyards Copper Moon 1999 Harvest White
Okanagan Valley VQA $8.95 (561266)
The moon was full when this blend of Pinot Gris and Chardonnay met. One thing led to another and soon it turned into a lovely match. Highlighted with honeydew melon and pear flavours, the fruit rides this medium-bodied white through to the finish.

Mission Hill Estate Winery 49 North 1999

Okanagan Valley VQA $12.95 (532853)

The consumer-friendly 49 North from Mission Hill is built for the cottage getaway. Flavours of banana and melon dominate this blend of Chardonnay, Pinot Blanc and Sémillon through to the finish. A touch of oak doesn't interfere too much with the fruit. Pairs well with suntan lotion, beach towels and sun.

Quails' Gate Estate Winery 2000 Chasselas/Pinot Blanc

Okanagan Valley VQA $12.95 (585737)

The characteristics of the hybrid Chasselas grape control the bouquet of this wine. Lemons and freshly cut grass make you think it's a Sauvignon Blanc. There's a slightly sweet touch on the palate with a nice lemon flavour that integrates well with the acids. Clean, crisp and refreshing, this one is built for patio dining.

RECOMMENDED

St. Hubertus Estate Winery 1999 Vintner's Reserve Okanagan Summer

Okanagan Valley VQA $9.35 (436709)

Talk about taking a walk on the wide side. This wine is a blend of Bacchus, Pinot Blanc and Chasselas. The mad mix has produced a surprisingly tasty treat. Pineapple, mango and bananas make for a great bouquet of tropical fruits. Light and lean on the palate, this is another blend that is meant for the patio or picnic.

Sumac Ridge Estate Winery 1999 Meritage (White)

Okanagan Valley VQA $18.95 (434977)

According to the regulations of the Meritage (pronounced like heritage) Association of America, White Meritage must be built with Sauvignon Blanc, Sémillon and Muscadelle. In this case, the Sauvignon Blanc dominates the nose as the gooseberry aromas wrestle with the oak. The oak subdues the fruit on the palate with pear and gooseberry waving the white flag. This wine could use a year or two in the cellar unless you're a fan of American oak. This would be a terrific match for smoked salmon, oysters and pot roast if you're looking for a white instead of a red.

Thirteenth Street Winery 2000 G.H. Funk Vineyards Musgeri

Niagara Peninsula $13

Sounds like an Italian food dish, but it's actually a blend of Muscat and Gewürztraminer. The two highly aromatic wines combine to create a lovely fragrance of rose petal, citrus and a touch of petrol. There's a level of acidity on the palate that would make it an ideal food-pairing wine. Suggested complements: pork chops and applesauce.

QUITE GOOD

L'Acadie 2000 Habitant

Nova Scotia $11.95

If you're on the East Coast and looking for some local wine—search this one out. A light and lean wine that smacks of a featherweight Riesling blended with Seyval Blanc. A bit of oak on the palate hides the citrus flavours. Quick finish—but could be a match for local seafood.

Mission Hill Estate Winery 1998 Cordillera Wild Horse Canyon

Okanagan Valley VQA $9.95 (574129)

After a long day of wrangling wild horses, this wine would be a nice treat while sitting around the campfire. Lemon drops and apple flavours would soften the most rugged of the cowboys. The fruit refreshes the palate with a surprisingly hot finish.

Pillitteri Estate Winery 1999 Gewürztraminer/Riesling

Niagara Peninsula VQA $10.95 (349126)

An interesting blend of two German varietals. Although a bit thick and cloying, ripe apple and tropical canned fruit highlight the wine from start to finish. A wine to try at the tasting bar just to see how two German wines get along.

St. Hubertus Winery Oak Bay Vineyard 1999 Grand Reserve Chardonnay/Pinot Blanc

Okanagan Valley VQA $12.95 (513721)

The Wonder Twins of blended whites have activated banana and pear powers to combat the oak monster. The duo leaves a lingering sweet trail of pears and cantaloupe.

Strewn Wines 1998 Two Vines Chardonnay/Pinot Blanc

Niagara Peninsula VQA $10.95 (587600)

This blend got in a tussle with some oak hooligans and lost the battle. Fruit manages to get off the ground on the palate, but oak rules the turf. For oak fans, give this one a try if you're at the winery.

Sparkling Wines

FOOD PAIRING SUGGESTIONS
Sparkling wine is still the best way to make an impression; serve it as an aperitif as your guests arrive.

There are a lot of sparkling wines made in Canada, including enormous vats of Baby Duck and other crackling pop wines made in bulk in giant wine factories. The presence of those so-called sparklers makes it difficult for producers of serious fizz to catch a break. But some estate wineries are staring down the stigma of Moody Blue and Baby Duck (which are more wine cooler than anything else) with exceptional sparklers that are as elegant and fun as the finest Champagne. For the record, only the French region of Champagne makes Champagne; everyone else makes sparkling wine.

Fundamental to the success of all good sparkling wines is a crisp, firm backbone of acidity, which can only be achieved in relatively cool climates. If, as has been tried in some warmer climates, the grapes are harvested earlier, the acidity can be preserved, but this generally does not permit the required flavour to develop in the grapes.

That said, Canada's cool-climate wine regions are a natural for sparkling wine production. Vintners are using Riesling, Chardonnay, Pinot Noir and Pinot Meunier to produce stylish and flavourful wines. Two winemaking methods are generally employed. The Charmat process, or method cuve close, sees the wine undergo secondary fermentation in a reinforced stainless steel tank. The more rarefied traditional method has the second fermentation taking place in the bottle in which the wine is sold. This is the quality method, which produces tiny pearl string bubbles in the wine. Some of the wines reviewed might be difficult for consumers to find because they sell out quickly and then disappear until the next vintage. The labour-intensive process means only small lots are produced each year.

—LB, RP, WS, CW

VINES AWARD

Sumac Ridge Estate Winery 1997 Stellar's Jay

Okanagan Valley VQA $21.95 (264879)

It's as if there's a party in your mouth and everyone's invited. The delicate balance between the
trio of Pinot Blanc, Chardonnay and Pinot Noir
creates a rich and elegantly structured sparkler.
Aromas of straw, cherry vanilla and angel cake
coupled with a long finish make this bubbly a
delight. If we could party like it was 1999 again,
this would be a great one to pop the cork with.

HIGHLY RECOMMENDED

Hillebrand Estates Trius Brut N/V

Niagara Peninsula VQA $19.95 (451641)

This Trius entry also took top marks from the
panel. Based on the classic Champagne method
approach, this non-vintage sparkler captured all
the elements of well-made Champagne. From the
elegant string of pearl bubbles dancing in the
glass to the exceptional fizz and good yeasty
qualities, this sophisticated Champagne pretender
could stand up to many of the real McCoys.

Peller Estates Founder's Series Cristalle N/V

Niagara Peninsula VQA $24.95 (542142)

Cristalle's high ranking from the panel was based
on its uniquely Canadian spin. With a dosage of
Icewine added to the mix, this sparkler is given a
new and interesting flavour profile. Aromas of ripe
lychee and rosewater give it a Gewürztraminer
appeal. With its finely balanced body, the touch
of Icewine sweetness doesn't overpower the
wine. This would be a good sparkler to serve
before dessert.

RECOMMENDED

Château des Charmes Estate Winery 1996 Blanc de Noir

Niagara Peninsula VQA $29.95

Interesting aromas of candied fruit carry over onto the palate and add a curious charm to this fruity and dry vintage sparkler produced from 100 percent Pinot Noir. Medium-bodied with a slight bitterness, this charming wine is a mellow fellow with fine bubbles.

Thirteenth Street Winery 1999 Gunther Funk Vineyards Riesling Brut

Niagara Peninsula VQA $17

An aromatic and zesty sparkling wine that's modelled after a serious Sekt, Funk's vintage Riesling sparkler offers floral aromas and a lively and elegant mouth-feel with intense pear and apple flavours and green apple acidity. This expressive wine will complement a wide variety of foods and would add a certain polish to your Sunday brunch.

QUITE GOOD

Colio Estates 1998 Lily Cuve Close

Ontario VQA $13.95 (509083)

Always a crowd-pleaser, Colio's Lily is a light and lively sparkling wine. A fine sipping wine, this vintage is dry with supple fruit flavours and a slightly tart finish. If you're looking for a good sparkler for a wedding or anniversary party—this one's got the pop power.

Vineland Estates Winery 1999 Riesling Cuve Close

Ontario VQA $22.95

Vineland specializes in Riesling production so it should come as no surprise that its sparkling wine is created from Germany's noble white wine grape. Vineland's cuve, which underwent secondary fermentation in a reinforced stainless steel tank, unleashes a tart, citrus taste. Enjoyably fresh and a tad off-dry, this would be great for a summer beach party or picnic.

PINK WINE

ROSÉ

Like Panama hats, convertibles and that special anxiety about losing weight before going to the beach, rosé wine is an integral part of summer. And the days of drinking sweet, cheaply made rosé in the shade are fading as winemakers craft complex and elegant versions of this refreshing wine.

The opaque, pale colour is key to the enjoyment of rosés, which are gaining in popularity across Canada. Their hue and flavour depend largely on the production method and grape varieties used. One style blends finished red wine with finished white wine. The resulting colour is pink and the flavours are a complex blend of complementary characteristics. The more popular style comes from using dark-skinned grapes and limiting the amount of skin contact. The less time fermenting on the skins, the lighter the colour of the finished wine.

The result of both processes is a dry or off-dry wine refreshing enough to be enjoyed on

FOOD PAIRING SUGGESTIONS
The range in rosé styles from crisp to sweet means that not all rosés can be paired well with food. For a rule of thumb, if the rosé is noted as "dry," "crisp" or "slightly sweet," it could be paired with grilled white meats like chicken and pork or with fish. If the rosé leans toward the sweet side in style, it would best be enjoyed on its own or with a fruit dish—think strawberries and cream.

the stickiest August day, but with the appealing red fruit characteristics found in red wines.

Male insecurity about anything pink has allowed females to dominate the pleasures of the rosé market. If guys would stop talking about the torque of their BMWs (a word few men actually can define), they might realize that rosé is the wine for the modern man. Hell, Russell Crowe cried in *Gladiator*, fellows. Lighten up. Enjoy a glass of rosé.

—LB, GP, WS, CW, JW

VINES AWARD

Peninsula Ridge Estates 2000 Rosé
Niagara Peninsula VQA $10.95
Winemaker Jean Pierre Colas hasn't forgotten where he came from. The recently landed Frenchman has crafted a beautiful Cabernet Franc rosé in the style of a Cabernet d'Anjou from France. Bright aromatics and flavours of crushed raspberries are highlighted in this dry and tangy wine. It can be enjoyed on its own, but it's zesty enough to be a perfect match for grilled pork, chicken and fish or even nachos and salsa on the deck.

HIGHLY RECOMMENDED

Daniel Lenko Estate Winery 2000 Rosé
Niagara Peninsula VQA $12.95
A wine made for the *Love Boat*. As love swirls around the salty air on the *Pacific Princess*, Isaac Washington would be pouring this deliciously fragrant and gentle wine for those falling in love. Pleasant strawberry notes merge with highly perfumed aromas in this slightly sweet rosé that finishes with a lingering fruitiness that is so very appealing. Captain Stubing could have used this rosé on those lonely nights at sea between episodes.

Henry of Pelham Family Estate Winery 2000 Rosé

Niagara Peninsula VQA $10.95 (395897)

Pretty in pink: here's a clean, refreshing vintage with tempting red berry flavours and rose petal aromas. This is a fabulous sipping wine that would also pair nicely with grilled salmon or tuna, pasta salad and quiche.

Jackson-Triggs 1999 Blanc de Noir Rosé

Okanagan Valley VQA $12.95 (543850)

Here's a delicate but expressive rosé produced from Pinot Noir. Sweet strawberry fruit and a crisp acidity are two of the wine's most attractive characteristics. This is a dry rosé that's elegant enough to serve at the dinner table with your good china, but it's also casual enough for paper plates and your back deck. Dress it up; you can take it anywhere.

RECOMMENDED

Daniel Lenko Estate Winery 2000 White Merlot

Niagara Peninsula VQA $13.95

The faint salmon colour and lovely flavour of this vintage make it as romantic as Valentine's Day, a rooftop picnic and a Tom Hanks/Meg Ryan movie all rolled together. Fresh and fruity, this is summer in a glass.

Kacaba Vineyards 1999 Rebecca Rosé

Niagara Peninsula VQA $9.95

This pink wine is deceptively pale, but on the palate it's a mouthful. Some nice earthy and smoky notes add an interesting complexity to the mixed berry fruit flavours and vibrant acidity. Tasty in its own right, this wine really shines when paired with a meal. Think of it as being the stylish first course of an amazing spring dinner party.

Thomas & Vaughan Vintners Cabernet Rosé 2000

Niagara Peninsula VQA $11.95

A flavourful blend of Cabernet Sauvignon and Cabernet Franc, this crowd-pleasing rosé is a pleasant combination of smoky notes, berry and cherry fruit and a hint of sweetness. Pair with a Chinese stir-fry, grilled chicken and fish or summer salads—any cool pasta, fruit or vegetable variety will do.

QUITE GOOD

Cave Spring Cellars Dry 1999 Rosé

Niagara Peninsula VQA $10.95 (295006)

Earthy, meaty aromas detract somewhat from the perfumed strawberry notes in this dry Euro-chic rosé. Crisp and mouth-watering, this is a willing partner for your summer picnic or favourite deck chair.

EastDell Estates 1999 Winter Rosé

Ontario VQA $10.95

This medium-bodied, dry wine offering muted strawberry and citrus aromas is an agreeable blend of Vidal and Gamay Noir. Delicate and fair, it's an easygoing wine to enjoy by the glass.

Konzelmann Estate Winery 1999 Pinot Noir Rosé

Niagara Peninsula VQA $10.80 (200568)

Lively strawberry jam flavours jump out of the glass of this single varietal rosé. This off-dry wine rounds out with a plush, pretty and smooth finish. Chill and serve with freshly grilled steak burgers.

Larch Hills Winery 1999 Tamarack Rosé
Salmon Arm, B.C. $11.50 (595660)
This refreshing West Coast rosé offers intense
perfumed aromas, while on the palate some
smoky and herbal notes nicely complement its
refreshing red berry flavours.

Sumac Ridge Estate Winery
1999 Okanagan Blush
Okanagan Valley VQA $9.95 (136994)
Sumac Ridge has produced a proprietary blend
of red and white wines that is off-dry with low but
balanced acidity. The residual sugar makes this
more of a mellow sipping wine than a bottle to
bring to the dinner table. It lacks the crisp snap
of tanginess that complements summertime fare.

Thirty Bench Winery 2000 Trillium Blush
Niagara Peninsula $9.50
The aroma of this wine is a dead ringer for those
red, white and blue popsicles—remember those
icy cherry and strawberry wonders? Sweet and
refreshing, this is too sticky for the dinner table.
Poolside is more like it.

RED WINE

CABERNET FRANC

Cabernet Franc is one of the noble vinifera grape varieties particularly well suited to cool climate wine regions and is considered by many vintners to be Canada's great red hope. The hierarchy of Bordeaux red wines puts the leaner, more herbaceous Cabernet Franc a distant second to the heavyweight Cabernet Sauvignon. But it's another case of a child surpassing its parent. In 1997, DNA research confirmed Cabernet Franc and Sauvignon Blanc were the parents of Cabernet Sauvignon.

Cabernet Franc, whose buds mature more than a week earlier than Cabernet Sauvignon, is lighter in colour and tannins than its more fashionable offspring. However, it has similar or higher levels of acidity and the same sort of flavour and structure. Like other Bordeaux reds, its flavours tend more toward the salad bar

spectrum (most notably green pepper) than juicy red fruit. One can detect raspberry when it is under-ripe or over-cropped, although in warm vintages such as 1998 and 1999 the wine can showcase a layered fruitiness, which is extremely appealing.

Francly-speaking, the grape is better known globally as a blending agent than a one-grape wine. Adding Merlot and Cabernet Sauvignon helps fill in the holes of Cabernet Franc's lean structure to produce lush, mouth-filling wines. But the almost yearly success of one-grape Cabernet Franc in Ontario and British Columbia is nothing to shy away from.

The biggest hurdle to overcome is marketing. When consumers hear Cabernet, they assume Cabernet Sauvignon is the topic at hand. Cabernet Franc produces truly great wines in France, particularly in the Loire and St-Emilion regions, but those are labelled as appellation or château wines. Only those wine lovers with a bit of Sherlock Holmes in them know that what they are enjoying is premium Cabernet Franc.

The growing popularity of varietal Cabernet Franc in California will undoubtedly help cement the winning wine's reputation in the New World and help create a bigger market for these wonderful wines. Until then, consider yourself a pioneering force—the front line of Cabernet Franc fans who can reap the rewards of being the first on the bandwagon.

—RC, WH, SS, WS, CW

Peller Estates 1998 Andrew Peller Signature Series Cabernet Franc Barrel Aged

Niagara Peninsula VQA $42.95 (981134)

This Franc is classically styled like Sinatra—raw and refined. On one hand, there are unmistakably elegant aromas of chocolate, cherry and coffee, but the wine's whiff of charcoal and leather, bright tannins and broad shoulders contrast this tender side. A wonderfully structured wine, which would be good company for a big he-man dinner party featuring meat and potatoes and *Sinatra at the Sands* on the stereo, its full flavours are big, round and impressive. Mature notes of cedar and tobacco combine with a rich core of fruit flavours to make for a wine that'll please a wide variety of palates—from young lovers to older swingers.

Pillitteri Estates Winery 1999 Cabernet Franc Family Reserve

Niagara Peninsula VQA $44 (349209)

A textbook Cabernet Franc with expressive aromas of currants, chocolate, sweet tobacco, mint and cut grass, this is a full-bodied wine with a great future ahead of it. Like the cigar-chomping Baby Herman from *Who Framed Roger Rabbit?* this wine is deceptive. It's young but has an old soul. The sweet tobacco and currant notes carry over onto the palate and marry with smoke, spice and vanilla flavours and gripping youthful tannins. A rich, round red with some dry tannins yet to be shed, it's awash in pleasant mouth-watering acidity, which makes it the perfect partner for lamb, veal or savoury mushroom dishes. Decant for an hour or two before dinner or cellar this impressive red for two to four years to maximize its potential.

HIGHLY RECOMMENDED

Burrowing Owl Vineyards 1999 Cabernet Franc Estate Bottled

Okanagan Valley VQA $30 (556621)

Ripe fruit aromas (cherry and cassis) marry coffee and grassy notes in this medium-bodied red that delivers heavily extracted ripe blackberry and smoky flavours on the palate. Rich and young, this wine suffers from crisp acidity and youthful tannins that add an astringency to the finish. That rawness will be shed given some time in the bottle or by decanting this wine two or three hours before dinner.

D'Angelo Estate Wines 1998 Cabernet Franc Reserve

Lake Erie North Shore VQA $20 (554428)

The wine's subtle aromas of violets, currants and crushed leaves are deceptive. They prepare you for a leaner, meaner Cabernet Franc instead of this explosive rich and concentrated wine. Smoky characteristics blend with leather, sweet tobacco, spice, currants and green pepper flavours in this weighty wine that features a wonderful velvety mouth-feel. Only a decided lack of ripe fruit flavours kept this stunner off the *Vines* Award podium.

Hillebrand Estates 1998 Showcase Cabernet Franc Glenlake Vineyard Unfiltered

Niagara Peninsula VQA $40 (994582)

Inviting herbal, red fruit and red licorice aromas storm out of the glass, luring you to try this full-bodied red that continues to impress with its fruit and herbal flavours. Like the Toronto Raptors, this young wine has a lot of promising components that point to a bright future. It's enjoyable now, but given a couple of years to gel there's no telling how much better this wine will be. We predict a championship season in 2004.

Inniskillin Okanagan Wines 1998 Cabernet Franc Dark Horse Vineyards Estate Bottled

Okanagan Valley VQA $17.95 (558387)

This wine's floral and perfume aromas don't scream Cabernet Franc—it's more like breezing past Holt Renfrew's fragrance counter than a trip through the produce aisles. But the ripe fruit flavours and chewy tannins are off the charts. Round and full on the palate, this is a tasty big red.

Pillitteri Estates Winery 1999 Cabernet Franc

Niagara Peninsula VQA $19.95 (349241)

Here's the wine equivalent of Sylvester Stallone's *Rocky*. This massive and crisp Cabernet Franc has big tannins that'll clobber the toughest steak into submission. Tobacco and herbal aromas trade punches with spice and blackcurrant notes. The aggressive palate serves up some serious chin music—a bracing flurry of spice and pepper, leather, black cherry and blackcurrant flavours that ultimately deliver a knock-out wallop with the long, lingering finish. Time will make this less austere, allowing its soft core of fleshy fruit to triumph.

RECOMMENDED

Calona Vineyards Sandhill 1999 Cabernet Franc

Okanagan Valley VQA $15.95 (556935)

Sweetish fruit, especially cherry and cassis, and veggie aromas carry over onto the palate, which is enhanced by soft tannin and spice essence. Not overly complex, this is an attractive wine to be enjoyed during an elegant night around the dinner table.

Château des Charmes Estate Winery 1998 Cabernet Franc St. David's Bench

Niagara Peninsula VQA $24.95 (453415)

The wine's pronounced nose of floral, perfumed, cherry fruit is an open invitation to enjoy this layered and complex Cabernet Franc. Herbal notes peek through the core of ripe fruit flavours, while the crisp acidity and firm tannins add structure to this well-made wine.

Colio Estates Winery 1999 Cabernet Franc CEV Reserve

Lake Erie North Shore VQA $18.95 (432096)

Candied cherry, chocolate aromas and ripe fruit flavours make this Cabernet Franc something for the wine lover with a sweet tooth. The wine is dry and firm, but those luscious aromas will make you feel like a kid in a candy store.

Crown Bench Estates 1999 Cabernet Franc Vintners' Reserve Beamsville Bench Estate Bottled

Niagara Peninsula VQA $24.95

Oaky vanilla and some herbal scents make for a nice first impression, while the soft tannins and mouth-filling flavours seal the deal for this attractive red. Pair this with a choice cut of beef, soft candlelight and ambient music, and you will have a setting for instant romance in the dining room.

Daniel Lenko Estate Winery 1999 Cabernet Franc

Niagara Peninsula VQA $24.95

An aromatic wine with engaging vanilla and deep tobacco and leather scents, this Cabernet Franc is full on the palate with balanced acidity and firm tannins. A long, dry, lingering finish completes the pretty picture. Drinking well now, it has the potential to age over the next three to five years.

EastDell Estates 1999 Cabernet Franc Walnut Grove Vineyard

Niagara Peninsula VQA $14.95

Walnut Grove's most famous inhabitants, the Ingalls family of *Little House on the Prairie* might have been immune to the delicate charms of this youthful Cabernet Franc. But, we're betting the Olson family would have indulged in this red with its plum, cassis and candied aromas. The red fruit flavours and spicy finish makes the wine very approachable now, which is more than we can say for those Olsons.

Harrow Estates 1999 Cabernet Franc

Lake Erie North Shore VQA $9.95 (297184)

You won't need to use a lifeline to figure out this straightforward Cabernet Franc, which makes the most of its attractive chocolate, spice and subtle fruit aromas and flavours. The wine's herbal notes add some complexity on the palate. The finish is nice and long. This is a solid, well-made Cabernet Franc. Final answer.

Hillebrand Estates 1995 Showcase Cabernet Franc Unfiltered Glenlake Vineyard

Niagara Peninsula VQA $48 (994582)

Here's a mature Cabernet Franc that offers aromas of chocolate, spice and everything nice in an aged red wine. For those of you keeping score at home, the list includes leather, sweet tobacco, bread and mushrooms. Those earthy flavours carry over onto the palate and merge with some subtle currant fruit flavours for a nice layered mouthful. Drink now.

Hillebrand Estates 1997 Showcase Cabernet Franc Unfiltered Glenlake Vineyard

Niagara Peninsula VQA $40 (399980)

A big, burly wine with complex aromas and flavours of leather, hay, earth, green pepper and deep rich black fruit. Its suitably big tannins are in need of being tamed by Father Time. The wine has all the components of being a Highly Recommended classic once it mellows and integrates with some bottle age.

Inniskillin Wines 1998 Cabernet Franc Reserve

Niagara Peninsula VQA $18.95 (557264)

Colombian coffee grower Juan Valdez took a wrong turn and ended up in a Niagara vineyard. This wine is awash in coffee aromas and flavours—it's like vintage Maxwell House. A suitably big red, the wine's dusty tannins will soften, given some bottle age, to reveal a rich core of fruit and tasty spice and herbal flavours.

Lakeview Cellars 1999 Cabernet Franc

Niagara Peninsula VQA $19.95 (573220)

Another big red with loads of fruit and spice aromas and flavours, with earthy undertones and some chocolate. Flavourful and supple, its mouth-filling texture will make a lot of friends wherever it's poured.

Peller Estates 1998 Cabernet Franc Private Reserve

Niagara Peninsula VQA $19.95 (981209)

This dark, rich red wine, which spent a year hibernating in oak barrels, offers some green herbaceous notes along with the soft raspberry and black pepper aromas. The spice carries over on the palate of this premium Cabernet Franc, which is flavourful and very forthcoming with its lush cherry, raspberry and cassis fruit characteristics.

Southbrook Winery 1999 Cabernet Franc Lailey Vineyard

Niagara Peninsula VQA $24.95 (448357)

An oaky red with supple chocolate and cassis flavours that stand out, this wine has an impressive mouth-feel and a slightly warm finish due to a higher alcohol content. The overwhelming oak mellows out the plummy fruit, but for fans of big and brawny reds, this is one to look for.

Strewn Wines 1998 Cabernet Franc Martin's Vineyard

Niagara Peninsula VQA $34 (557207)

A Valentine's Day wine with romantic aromas of flowers and chocolate and a warm embrace of fruit and herbal flavours. Spice and coffee notes reveal themselves on the palate, and the coffee flavours turn to creamy mocha on the long, lingering finish.

Tinhorn Creek Vineyards 1998 Cabernet Franc

Okanagan Valley VQA $11.95 (530717)

The whiff and taste of lush blackberry fruit is featured front and centre in this soft and round Cabernet Franc. A vein of crisp tannin enriches this mellow mouthful, which is rounded out by lingering dryness on the finish.

QUITE GOOD

Calona Vineyards Artist Series 1999 Cabernet Franc

Okanagan Valley VQA $11.95 (581686)

A dry and lean Franc with herbal/cherry flavours and dried cherry notes on the short finish. Best enjoyed with food.

EastDell Estates 1999 Cabernet Franc
Niagara Peninsula VQA $12.95
Pleasant raspberry and cherry notes are found in the nose and on the palate of this soft and delicate Cab. Light and lean, the fruit combines with grassy/green pepper flavours to make for a nice dinner wine.

Kacaba Vineyards 1999 Cabernet Franc
Niagara Peninsula VQA $21.95
Herbaceous veggie and coffee aromas are complemented by herbal flavours and balanced acidity. This is a prime food wine, which would partner with beef or lamb dishes.

Magnotta Winery 1999 Limited Edition Cabernet Franc
Niagara Peninsula VQA $38.50
A lot more greens in this wine than fruit. From start to finish, there's a strong streak of green herbs that gives the wine a youthful appeal. Herbaceous notes give way to some firm, youthful tannins on the palate. Bell peppers carry the flavour profile through to the finish with some undercurrents of cassis and black currants giving the wine an added depth. A crisp, slightly hot finish has the wine lingering a bit. Suggest an hour of decanting before serving—or let this limited edition rest a while in the cellar.

Nichol Vineyard 1998 Cabernet Franc Unfiltered Estate Bottled
Okanagan Valley $21.90 (572073)
A big and aggressive red with crushed leaf, smoke and herbal scents. A medium-bodied Cab, it features ripe black cherry, spicy and smoky flavours on the palate along with some firm tannin. For best effect, hold for two or three years before serving.

Pelee Island Winery 1999 Cabernet Franc
Pelee Island VQA $9.95 (433714)
This aromatic wine with its wafts of vegetables, black pepper and spice and smoke and vanilla flavours will be a crowd-pleaser once the astringent tannins mellow. There's some dryness in the finish, which currently borders on bitterness. Best buy for the price.

Stonechurch Vineyards 1998 Cabernet Franc
Niagara Peninsula VQA $18.95 (891051)
Like a strawberry social on the lawn of your local church, this elegant wine delivers berry, grassy and slight smoke flavours. Its subtle aromas and high acidity suggest this wine is hiding its true nature. Maybe it'll let down its hair a little once the priest is out of earshot.

Stoney Ridge Cellars 1998 Cabernet Franc Reserve
Niagara Peninsula VQA $11.95 (433524)
A light style of Cabernet Franc that might remind some of Pinot Noir, Stoney Ridge's wine is deceivingly pale. And the floral and sweet fruit aromas do little to give an inkling of the great mouth-filling flavours you'll get with the first sip. On the palate, there's pleasant cherry/raspberry flavours with some complex herbal and earthy notes.

Strewn Wines 1999 Cabernet Franc
Niagara Peninsula VQA $17.95 (557199)
Call this a future consideration. Subtle fruit and dusty berry aromas peek out, while subdued fruit flavours are present amid chalky young tannins. Opening this today would be a crime, but given two to four years to mellow, this should reward your patience with a killer Cabernet Franc.

Sumac Ridge Estate Winery 1998
Cabernet Franc Black Sage Vineyard

Okanagan Valley VQA $15.95 (392381)
Cherry pie and stewed fruit aromas suggest an
incoming fruit bomb, but the palate doesn't
match the nose. Herbal flavours, including green
pepper and mint, step to the forefront. The finish
is long and very pleasant.

CABERNET SAUVIGNON

In the world of red wine, Cabernet Sauvignon is afforded the same fanatical popularity Chardonnay enjoys over less fashionable white whites. Cabernet Sauvignon is the reigning heavyweight champion of the world and has beaten down all competitors for decades now.

For many wine lovers, Cabernet Sauvignon is red wine to the exclusion of everything else on the wine list. We have California to thank for that. The surfer girls and surfer boys have turned the world onto one-grape Cabernet wines that deliver arousing fruit explosions on the palate. That movement has inspired many New World winemakers, including a strong Canadian contingent, to follow in their "go big or go home" wake.

But their Old World counterparts in Bordeaux continue to see the aristocratic grape variety as the King of Kings. Cabernet Sauvignon is the

FOOD PAIRING SUGGESTIONS
The full-bodied red is a superb match for most meat dishes, everything from roast beef, lamb and veal to a wild kingdom of caribou and duck. Vegetarians need not despair; powerful Cabernet is also an impressive partner with vegetable stews and mushroom risotto.

principal ingredient in their world-renowned blended reds, which often include smaller portions of Merlot, Cabernet Franc, Malbec and a few other earthy vinifera grapes.

A hearty grapevine with particularly hard wood, Cabernet Sauvignon thrives in vineyards in British Columbia and Ontario. Surviving the winter is rarely a problem, but getting the late-ripening grapes to full maturity can be. In exceptionally cold and difficult years, the wines can be weedy and hard, but in fine vintages, they are delicious and wonderfully versatile. With back-to-back warm weather vintages, the *Vines* panel saw the best possible face of Canadian Cabernet Sauvignon.

Like the French approach, Cabernet Sauvignon's main use in both provinces is as a blending agent for Cabernet-Merlot or Meritage wines. But given the beneficial growing conditions and in the right hands, 100-percent Cabernet Sauvignon wines are some of the best red wines being produced in Canada. Classic Cabernet Sauvignon characteristics include cassis, red currants, cranberry, mint, eucalyptus, black cherry, bell pepper and smoke.

—JI, TK, WH, WS, CW

HIGHLY RECOMMENDED

Hillebrand Estates 1998 Cabernet Sauvignon Glenlake Vineyard Unfiltered
Niagara Peninsula VQA $40 (994566)
When wine lovers call for a Cab, this is the big, brawny drink they expect to pull up to the table. Some salad bar aromas mix with the cassis, cedar and mint notes that carry over to the palate. There is elegance behind the power of this full-throttle wine, thanks to the taming influence of the French oak in which it was aged. The flavours are dry; the texture is soft, warm and inviting.

Lakeview Cellars 1999 Cabernet Sauvignon

Niagara Peninsula VQA $24.95 (307173)

Many young Cabernet Sauvignons are mean and stand-offish, but this rich, concentrated and fruit-packed wine is a kinder, gentler Cab. A pleasantly spicy, creamy-textured wine with plenty of upfront fruit and admirable length, it is so good now there's no reason to let it age. It would be perfect with burgers, pizza or pasta, but it's classy enough to serve with more serious meat dishes.

Peller Estates 1998 Cabernet Sauvignon Private Reserve

Niagara Peninsula VQA $22 (981183)

Looking for a bottle to yank the feet from underneath that wine bore uncle who says Canada can't produce great red wine? This is it. Peller Estates' Reserve is a penetrating wine with tremendous length on the palate. It's accessible now and will be even better in two or three years when the fruit, oak and ripe tannins are more seamlessly integrated. This would be wonderful with stew, risotto or grilled red meat.

RECOMMENDED

Daniel Lenko Estate Winery 1999 Warren Private Reserve Cabernet Sauvignon

Niagara Peninsula VQA $39.95

A mellow mouthful, this Cab is especially impressive because of its structure, length and intensity. Its bright acidity and sweet currant and blackberry flavours make it an easy choice for steak or grilled portobellos.

Hillebrand Estates 1997 Cabernet Sauvignon Glenlake Vineyard Unfiltered

Niagara Peninsula VQA $42 (994566)

Soft and ripe with fascinating, earthy aromas, this maturing Cab has deftly concealed acidity and tannin that add weight and complexity. Partner this with well-seasoned pork, veal or chicken, meat-based pasta sauces or simple roast beef.

Jackson-Triggs 1998 Proprietors' Reserve Cabernet Sauvignon

Okanagan Valley VQA $19.95 (543884)

Canada's cool-climate wine regions produce brighter, fresher, more delicate wines than hot-house California's big, bold Cabs, which are as obvious as a Hollywood blockbuster. By comparison, Jackson-Triggs' wine is a great Canadian film: full of intrigue, plot and gripping characters. Who would you rather spend your evening with: Adam Sandler or Atom Egoyan?

Magnotta Winery 1999 Cabernet Sauvignon

Niagara Peninsula VQA $11.95

A rich, robust Cabernet Sauvignon that has the body of a heavyweight contender. Although it opens up with a soft black currant and blueberry combo, it's the weight on the palate that gives this wine its personality. With some heavy tannins and flavours, which include coffee, cedar, raspberry and blueberry, this wine has the complexity to stand its ground. Although still a bit youthful, with a little age it should be a dandy.

Peller Estates 1998 Andrew Peller Signature Series Cabernet Sauvignon

Niagara Peninsula VQA $45 (981126)

A strong meaty element pervades this well-crafted, impeccably made red wine, which would make your favourite cut of meat sing. A serious Cab built for the cellar, this young toughie should be decanted for three or four hours if you're considering serving it prior to, say, Christmas 2003.

Strewn Wines 1998 Cabernet Sauvignon Terroir Strewn Vineyard

Niagara Peninsula VQA $23.95 (557082)
A classic Cab with a trademark whiff and taste of cedar and cassis, this is a bottle for the less-is-more wine consumer. Anyone who appreciates smaller, more delicate wines over whopping ones that hammer the senses with intense aromas and flavours will love this wine's seductive whisper.

Strewn Wines 1999 Cabernet Sauvignon Terroir Strewn Vineyard

Niagara Peninsula VQA $23.95 (557082)
This full-bodied single-vineyard Cab offers exceptional, intense, blackberry fruit aromas with hints of cherry and mint. Pull the cork a couple of hours before you're due at the dinner table and this will be superb company for pizza, pasta, grilled steaks, lamb or stews.

QUITE GOOD

Calona Vineyards Artist Series 1999 Cabernet Sauvignon

Okanagan Valley VQA $12.95 (505248)
Here's a straightforward wine that will spice up a weekday meal. Delicious black cherry fruit and just the right touch of oak make for a simple but stylish Cab.

Calona Vineyards Copper Moon 1999 Harvest Cabernet Sauvignon

Okanagan Valley VQA $13.95 (580936)
Nice cherry and currant fruit with well-integrated wood spice—a winner with food.

Hernder Wines 1998 Cabernet Sauvignon

Niagara Peninsula VQA $28.95 (432559)
Lightly herbal flavours merge with fleshy black fruit on the palate of this wine, which is delightfully juicy but finishes short.

Southbrook Winery 1999 Cabernet Sauvignon Lailey Vineyard

Niagara Peninsula VQA $24.95 (448340)

A burly Cab with a firm tannic backbone, this is fascinating but controversial wine. Some tasters loved the wine's heft; others said the hard tannin steamrolled the fruit flavours. Everyone agreed this gripping wine would develop into a better drink given two or three years to mellow.

Stonechurch Vineyards 1999 Cabernet Sauvignon

Niagara Peninsula VQA $12.45 (353318)

A classic barbecue wine to serve with chicken, steak or pork chops. It is particularly well suited to grilled foods; the wine's ripe, seemingly sweet berry fruit contrasts nicely with the flavours imparted by the grill.

Sumac Ridge Estate Winery 1998 Cabernet Sauvignon Black Sage Vineyard

Okanagan Valley VQA $19.95 (392373)

The wine's sweet and fruity aromas and flavours are attractive, but its hard tannin and shorter finish require food for balance.

Thomas & Vaughan Vintners 1999 Cabernet Sauvignon

Niagara Peninsula VQA $16.95

A modestly proportioned wine with delicate flavours that are harmonious and enjoyable. This light-bodied wine is ready to drink now with food.

CABERNET BLENDS

To best describe the reason winemakers blend red varieties, we decided to pull a buzzword from the business pages of the daily newspapers—convergence. For some varieties, most notably Cabernets Franc, Sauvignon and Merlot, there is a synergy of flavours and structure that produce a better, fuller wine than any one-grape wine. The sum is, indeed, better than its parts.

There is, however, no formula, no secret recipe for vintners to follow when blending red wines. Winemakers must sweat out the process, tasting every barrel in the cellar individually to produce their vintage wine. Bordeaux winemakers have been blending Cabernet and Merlot, along with Malbec and Petit Verdot, for centuries, which is why some Canadian wineries refer to their red blends as "Bordeaux blends." The French figured out long ago that working with a variety of compatible grapes is the best insurance against disease and uneven ripening in the vineyard. The winemaker then has the flexibility to blend the

FOOD PAIRING SUGGESTIONS
Blended reds offer a more diverse package for pairing with foods. Many of the wines reviewed in this section would be best suited for hearty meals. From stews and chili to steaks and roasts, most red meats would stand up to the blends. As well, some of the lighter blends could be paired with white meat like pork and lamb. For vegetarians, try spicy pastas or grilled veggies with a nice hearty red.

harsh tannins and acidity of underripe Cabernets with the softer and richer flavours of Merlot, which ripens much earlier in the season. The percentage of each variety changes from year to year to reflect the strong suits of every vintage.

It should be noted here that Canadian blended reds consistently outshine stand-alone Merlot or Cabernet Sauvignon. We hope that more wineries will turn to blending to make the very best big reds instead of focusing so much attention on stand-alone varietals, which need exceptionally warm growing seasons to thrive. The process isn't confusing, but the wine labelling practice invariably is. Why are some wines labelled as Meritage, while some are Cabernet-Merlot and others still are given proprietary names like Nota Bene, Trius Red or Reserve Blend? Good question, and one that Canadian winemakers should address so the system can be demystified for confused consumers.

For the record, Meritage is a term minted by a California collective, which has set out stringent guidelines for wineries who want to use the designation. To obtain a licence and use that term, the wine must be a blend of two or more of the following varieties: Cabernet Franc, Cabernet Sauvignon, Merlot, Malbec, Petit Verdot, Gros Verdot, St. Macaire or Carmenere. No single variety can make up more than 90 percent of the blend.

—RD, WH, WS, CW, JW

Cabernet-Merlot Blends

VINES AWARD

Southbrook Winery 1998 Triomphe Cabernet-Merlot
Niagara Peninsula VQA $27.95 (533299)
This wine belongs in the old cotton clubs of the 1930s and '40s with Ella Fitzgerald singing the blues.

Built to transcend the ages like Ella's music, this big, robust red opens with a puff of smoke and leather. Soft, silky tannins coat the palate with smoky tobacco and cassis fruit adding a touch of sweetness to the finish. Let this one age for a couple more years, then match it with big gamey meats.

HIGHLY RECOMMENDED

Cave Spring Cellars 1999 Cabernet-Merlot
Niagara Peninsula VQA

Make way for the great Cabernet and Merlot duo. These wonders of the wine world have come together for just one night to perform magical tricks like combining raspberry and vanilla and adding a sweet touch to the finish. As you dig into your big, juicy steak, you'll wish you could have a repeat performance of the Cave Spring Cellars Cabernet-Merlot.

CedarCreek Estate Winery 1998 Cabernet-Merlot
Okanagan Valley VQA $16.95 (450650)

The offering from CedarCreek is absolutely delicious. Basket upon basket of cherries and currants wash over the senses. Built like a 100-year-old cedar, this full-bodied and finely structured red has the tannins to muscle it through some years, but it also possesses a subtle softness that makes it a pleasure to drink after an hour in the decanter.

Henry of Pelham Family Estate Winery 1998 Cabernet-Merlot
Niagara Peninsula VQA $29.95 (395855)

This wine is not ready to be enjoyed just yet. That said, a little while in the glass and lush notes of sweet cherries and ripe currants begin to dance around. The hard tannins start to loosen some strings and before long the sleeping monster starts to awaken. Although not really enjoyable in its youth, it is secure in its role as a major contender in the red blend category.

Konzelmann Estate Winery 1998 Cabernet-Merlot Reserve

Niagara Peninsula VQA $29.95 (897454)

Although a bit shy, once this reserve blend is let out to play, it start to display some of its finer characteristics. The fragrance is muted, even after some time in the glass, but the real telltale sign of craftsmanship comes on the palate. The complexity of the wine shows itself in the big red fruits that are surrounded by layers of leather and oak. The tannins are firm, but not intrusive. If the indicators are right, this one will be a winner in a few years.

Southbrook Winery 1999 Triomphe Cabernet-Merlot

Niagara Peninsula VQA $27.95 (533299)

Not as robust as its older sibling, the '99 red blend from Southbrook has the trademark smoky fragrance with a lot more vanilla and oak added to the mix. A dollop of vanilla on the palate is chased away with some sweet cherry and cassis. The tannins are a little tight right now, but with some aging or decanting, they should soften and coat the palate like a silk scarf. Big, gamey fare would be the match for this majestic red.

Vineland Estates Winery 1998 Reserve Cabernet-Merlot

Niagara Peninsula VQA $35

This one almost made it to the *Vines* Award podium. A hallmark wine from the class of '98, this Cabernet-Merlot has all the right stuff. Rich, dark chocolate and tobacco notes hint of some-thing delicious to come. The cherry and plum flavours are finely integrated with the soft oak on the palate. A deft touch by the winemaker has brought out the best of the fruit, without going over the edge. The spicy touch on the finish caps off a great wine. Any cellar would be proud to host this wine.

RECOMMENDED

Calona Vineyards Sandhill 1999 Cabernet Sauvignon-Merlot

Okanagan Valley VQA $15.95 (541144)

Although this wine is big enough to kick sand in the face of lesser blends, it has a soft side that would appeal to Frankie Avalon fans. Surf's up as raspberry and strawberry ride the wave in true *Muscle Beach Party* fashion. Upfront tannins add some complexity to the wine, but the finish ends on just the right note. If you're hanging out à la Frankie and Annette Funicello, slap some meat on the grill and uncork this one as the sun goes down.

Cave Spring Cellars 1998 Cabernet-Merlot

Niagara Peninsula VQA $30 (316943)

All-you-can-eat salad bar is the feature of the day with this blend. Green pepper dominates the herbaceous nose with some ground pepper adding some spice to the dish. Twists of pepper and tobacco weave their way through the wine to the finish. A little tart, but with some decanting and with leaner red meats and grilled veggies as accompaniments, this wine will be right at home.

Hillebrand Estates 1998 Collectors' Choice Merlot-Cabernet

Niagara Peninsula VQA $15.95 (566240)

Sounds like a coffee—"Collector's Choice, good to the last drop." Whatever the name, this Merlot leading blend is all about cherries. A sweet cherry touch on the palate gives the wine a pleasant, soft structure, leaving some of the pepper and oak traits in the dust. A lighter-styled red, it is drinking well now. Add this one to the collection.

Mission Hill Estate Winery 1999 Cabernet-Merlot

Okanagan Valley VQA $14.95 (257816)

Another friendly red that is drinking well now. Red berry fruits are wrapped in soft peppery

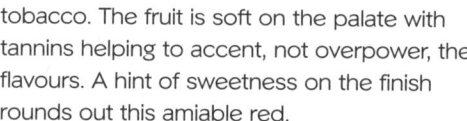

tobacco. The fruit is soft on the palate with tannins helping to accent, not overpower, the flavours. A hint of sweetness on the finish rounds out this amiable red.

Pelee Island Winery 1999 Cabernet-Merlot Vinedressers

Pelee Island VQA $14.95 (435321)

If "Vinedressers" refers to the crew that tends to the vines, they did a great job getting the fruit out of their vines in 1999. Huge plum and black-currant flavours swim around the huge tannins that seem to linger in the glass forever. An extended finish with a hot pinch at the end rounds out this wine. Kudos to the vinedresser for getting the fruit ready for the big dance. This red wouldn't feel out of place at a large wedding.

Meritage/Other Cabernet Blends

VINES AWARD

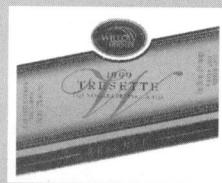

Willow Heights Winery 1999 Tresette Reserve

Niagara Peninsula VQA $24.95

A true testament of this wine is that it stood out in a group of wines that was largely very well built. This award winner has been bestowed with a complex bouquet of smoky tobacco that is rounded out with earthy black cherry and bell pepper fragrances. A touch of sweetness from the oak hits the palate first, followed by a splash of cherry and raspberry. A slight peppery finish caps off a finely blended wine. The success of this red blend continues to illustrate that Canadian red blends may be the future for red wine. Although drinking well know, a few years among the peasants in the cellar may give this wine even more regal powers.

HIGHLY RECOMMENDED

Creekside Estates Winery 1999 Laura's Blend

Niagara Peninsula VQA $17.95

One of the hallmark wines from Creekside, Laura's Blend shows the power of blending red wines. A robust red, the bouquet offers intense aromas of tobacco, leather and blueberries. Once on the palate, the wine lets loose with a torrent of luscious fruit led by blueberry and smothered in vanilla and tobacco. A deft hand with the oak provides a small dose of sweetness that intensifies the fruit without going over the top. With a nice rounded, fruity finish, Laura would be a great companion to any red meat dishes.

Daniel Lenko Estate Winery 1999 Meritage

Niagara Peninsula VQA $29.95

Deep oak, ripe fruit and marmalade aromas set the table for a fruity red that thrives with expressive chocolate and black fruit flavours. Its evolved palate explodes—dense fruit, sweet oak and silky tannins take flight in the wine's full-throttled flavour profile. Time should knit these layers more seamlessly, producing a rich, suave Meritage. The panel was confused when it came to pairing this wine with an ideal food. Serve it as dinner was one solution. Serve with chocolate fondue, soufflé desserts and after dinner cheese were more temperate options.

Inniskillin Okanagan Wines 1998 Meritage Dark Horse Vineyards

Okanagan Valley VQA $19.95 (558395)

Big and fleshy like Elvis in the 1970s, this classic blend is a bona fide hunka, hunka-burning love. Raspberry jam and chocolate aromas are all shook up with pepper and licorice notes. Those crowd pleasingly rich and ripe fruits work up a sweat on the palate, karate chopping their way through a velvet fog of cedar, smoke and old leather. A very fruity, delicious wine with balanced acidity and pleasant mouth-feel and aftertaste,

this is the Meritage that would be King. It'll take care of business in any setting. Impress friends, family and business colleagues. The fans are sure to go wild... Thank you, thank you very much.

Inniskillin Wines 1998 Meritage Reserve
Niagara Peninsula VQA $19.95 (557272)
This wine is smokin'—as Jim Carrey exclaimed in the movie *The Mask*. With wafts of tobacco, cigar box and cherry vanilla jostling for your attention, this is a happening wine. On the palate, the party continues with massive doses of ripe berries cutting some serious rug with chic leather and tobacco types. With the party raging into the night, this wine lingers well after the sun comes up. Although this wine can mingle with the in crowd now, it will be an extremely cool cat in a few years time.

Pillitteri Estates Winery 1999 Trivalente
Niagara Peninsula VQA $39.95 (349225)
A delicious wine that offers a twist on the old Reese's Peanut Butter Cups commercial: "You've got black pepper in my chocolate! You've got chocolate in my black pepper!" Two great tastes that taste great together, indeed. The mellow cocoa and spice notes perk up the concentrated fruit aromas and flavours. Cedar and tobacco also join in the fray. This medium-to-full-bodied wine is flavourful enough to serve with a cheese course and inspire great discussions about poetry and politics, but can also nuzzle up to a main course of lamb, mushroom risotto or pasta with tomato sauce.

RECOMMENDED

Black Hills Estate Winery 1999 Nota Bene
British Columbia $28.00 (708073)
Roberto Beninni would be proud of this *Nota Bene*. A big, smokey Canadian posing as an Italian has lots of leather and tobacco notes that point toward a big, bold offering. On the palate,

the leather chaps make a splash with a dash of black pepper. Although the tannins are a bit firm, this one has the heft to challenge time. Life is indeed beautiful.

Hillebrand Estates 1999 Trius Red
Niagara Peninsula VQA $19.95 (303800)
The same way Pierre Elliot Trudeau illuminated Parliament Hill with culture, grace and youth in 1969, this toddler seems destined to eke out its own impressive legacy. A classically styled red, it's restrained in its youth, offering only the subtlest hints of cherry, cedar and spice on the nose. The wine unfolds on the palate—lush layers of wonderfully polished fruit and nicely integrated oak assert themselves while cedar, chocolate, tobacco and mint wait in the wings. Full-bodied and intense, all will be revealed in years to come—just watch.

Jackson-Triggs 1998 Proprietors' Grand Reserve Meritage
Niagara Peninsula VQA $24.95 (563189)
Never mind the Grand Reserve designation, this bouncing baby Bordeaux blend was designed with the dinner table in mind. A lovely wine that's full of fruit, it offers deep plummy flavours and a lingering cedary raspberry note on the finish. The whiff and taste of black pepper and earth adds some depth to this soft wine, which has a slight tannic grip that gives it the right stuff to stare down a choice cut of beef or veal. Serve blind to a table of family and friends for best results and see if anyone can guess this fleshy, ripe and expressive wine was made in Canada.

Maleta Estate Winery 1999 Meritage
Niagara Peninsula VQA $24.95
A charmer with silky tannins and beguiling aromas of licorice and smoke, this wine is low keyed at first blush. Given time to smolder, however, the embers of subtle fruit and spice catch fire. Deep and lovely, this offers a good fruity mouthful of

flavours that would pair nicely with bistro fare such as steak and frites or prime rib.

Peninsula Ridge Estates Winery 1999 Reserve Meritage

Niagara Peninsula VQA $39.95

Impressive at this young stage, this wine is round and soft, rather like the cocoon that disguises the magical metamorphosis of a breathtaking breed of butterfly. Some herbal salad and tobacco notes mingle with the core of ripe red fruit flavours, which adds complexity and depth to this intoxicating wine. Those rich, deep flavours will mellow and better integrate to yield a finer wine in two to three years. In other words, wait for the video release.

Strewn Wines 1999 Terroir Strewn Three

Niagara Peninsula VQA $24.95 (468918)

Nicely refined with very good fruit flavour, this understated youngster is a bit like listening to Nirvana *Unplugged.* Deep and concentrated, the subtle toasty and spice aromas are quiet now but you just know they're going to burst into a full-throated scream given time. Mind you, this isn't a blockbuster fruit bomb. A wine of grace and power, it is balanced and offers a glimpse of a Bordeaux-blend at its ingenuous best.

Sumac Ridge Estate Winery 1998 Meritage Black Sage Vineyard

Okanagan Valley VQA $25.00 (392399)

If a cedar tree falls in the forest, can you smell it? If you want a reference tool, uncork this offering from Sumac Ridge. Full of cedar and black cherries on the nose, the wine becomes even livelier on the palate. Flavours of cherries and red currants are enhanced by the subtle touch of oak that acts as a foundation from which the fruit shines. A hint of oak sweetness on the finish accents a fine wine that would pair well with smoked sea fare or grilled red meats.

MERLOT

There were two bottles on the table, one was a Merlot, the other was a Cabernet, and at the end of the night there were three bottles of the Merlot left. I tell ya, Merlot gets no respect! Merlot is the Rodney Dangerfield of the wine world, forever being passed over for Cabernet—Franc and Sauvignon.

The role that has been assigned to Merlot is that of supporting cast. In France, Merlot is widely planted, not to be produced as a single varietal but to support the Bordeaux blends, which include Cabernet Sauvignon, Cabernet Franc and Merlot. Forever living in the shadow of the Cabernet giants, Merlot counters the highly tannic structure of the Cabernet Sauvignon, and its supple fruit and sweeter characteristics balance the Cabernets to make the blended red approachable in its youth.

FOOD PAIRING SUGGESTIONS
The more complex, full-bodied Merlots go well with red meats. The lighter styled versions are good companions with pork roasts, duck, quail and other game birds.

In Canada, Merlot is living a double life. The early flowering and ripening characteristics of the varietal make it an appealing red grape to produce. Widely grown in both British Columbia and Ontario, wineries are using the grape as both a blending wine and for single varietal production. The consistent success of its blending capabilities can be witnessed in the Cabernet Blends section of the book. As a one-grape wine, the results vary widely.

On its own, a well-made Merlot can display supple fruit—black cherries, cassis and raspberries—with a touch of sweetness. It can handle oak, and, if a deft hand is used in the process, chocolate and tobacco mingle with the fruit giving the wine more complexity. In the warmer growing conditions of the 1998 vintage, the grapes were able to reach great depths of maturity and when handled properly were built into wonderfully integrated wines. In cooler seasons, it's much more difficult to handle. Indeed, the jury is out on domestic Merlot's ability to take a leading role. Still, there are bright spots where Merlot shines, and an exceptional supporting role is just as important as carrying a film alone.

—MA, LB, WS, CW

VINES AWARD

The panel couldn't pick a winner between these two wines for our Merlot *Vines* Award, which is interesting considering the different winemaking philosophies at play. Hillebrand's winner is made in a classic Old World fashion, big and round with complex characteristics, while the Jackson-Triggs wine delivers a depth charge of explosive fruit flavours. In their own particular way, these wines represented the best Merlots put before our panel.

Hillebrand Estates 1998 Showcase Merlot Glenlake Vineyard

Niagara Peninsula VQA $40 (994574)

There's a sophisticated and sensual air about this impressive wine that's as timeless and riveting as Fellini's classic *La Dolce Vita*. The wine's pronounced aromas—chocolate, oak spice and green pepper—are time-honoured Bordeaux hallmarks. On the palate the wine's full body, rich cherry flavours and lovely finish are equally compelling.

Jackson-Triggs 1998 Proprietors' Grand Reserve Merlot

Niagara Peninsula VQA $19.95 (563197)

A thoroughly modern wine with loads of impressive fruit aromas and flavours and a round, plush mouth-feel, Jackson-Triggs' wine is fresh and inspiring—like Sam Mendes' Academy Award winner *American Beauty*. Like the film, this wine tells a gripping story with layers of seductive fruit and complex coffee and toffee notes.

HIGHLY RECOMMENDED

Burrowing Owl Vineyards 1999 Merlot

Okanagan Valley VQA $25 (509885)

From the land of the Owl comes a youthful Merlot with a lot of potential. Although shy in displaying its aromas, the body of this wine shows off its inner beauty. The key description for this wine's high ranking is integration. It's a medium-bodied red with subtle nuances of passion fruit ice cream and a hint of raspberry. Solid, firm tannins hold the weight through the finish with a bit of a hot spike at the end. The deft hand displayed at integrating the oak and fruit will carry this wine for years to come. Best enjoyed after a few years in the cellar.

Daniel Lenko Estate Winery 1999 Old Vines Merlot

Niagara Peninsula VQA $24.95

Huge wafts of chocolate fill the air. Spoonfuls of chocolate with ripe cassis and cherries swirl about this mouth-watering Merlot. Soft and round tannins give it structure without being too intrusive. Although it will develop with age, this is a very approachable Merlot. Pairing mates include big, meaty dinners or rich pasta sauces.

Jackson-Triggs 1999 Proprietors' Reserve Merlot

Okanagan Valley VQA $16.95 (543876)

Another Merlot that's built to dwell in the cellar for a few years. Consumers of wine-ready-to-drink-now should be warned not to unleash this wine—it's not ready. The subdued nose is the first indication that the wine is still in its infancy. Although oak dominates the palate, the presence of black cherries and cassis behind the wood needs only time to come together. After a while in the glass, this red opens up beautifully. All the seeds of a great Merlot are present, it just needs time to find itself.

Kacaba Vineyards 1999 Merlot

Niagara Peninsula VQA $14.95

It's like taking a tour of Willy Wonka's chocolate factory. The tour starts with a rich fragrance of dark chocolate with mocca coffee. Next up, there's vanilla and chocolate on the palate that rides the assembly line toward a finely designed finish. A slightly spicy ending keeps you focused on the tour. A perfect match for seasoned red meats on the grill.

Mission Hill Estate Winery 1999 Merlot Reserve

Okanagan Valley VQA $22.95 (553313)

Memories of going to the corner store to buy those 5¢ cherry Twizzlers come racing back with a sniff of Mission Hill's Reserve Merlot. Expressive cherry and raspberry aromas capture the essence of the fruit. A medium-bodied offering, the sweet touch of oak on the palate integrates well with the ripe fruit flavours. Hangs around for a while before heading home. Ideal for tomato-based pasta dishes.

Peller Estates 1998 Andrew Peller Signature Series Merlot

Niagara Peninsula VQA $42 (981142)

This wine was a contender for the *Vines* Award, and Andrew Peller, founder of Andrés Wines, would be very proud of this Merlot. The intense fragrance conjures up an image of standing in a cedar forest enjoying a chocolate bar. It's a big, bold red with plenty of soft, round tannins. Although it trips on the finish because of its youth—this is a big Merlot that will age gracefully. Best enjoyed in five to 10 years.

Pillitteri Estates Winery 1999 Family Reserve Merlot

Niagara Peninsula VQA $22.95 (349209)

Imagine having a rich mocca coffee and swirling a piece of toffee around in it. That's where this wine is now. Full-bodied without the invasive tannins, the oak steers the flavours on the palate uncovering red currants and cranberries around the bend. Although a bit short on the finish, it's a well-crafted Merlot. Try this with pork roast or roasted chicken.

RECOMMENDED

Château des Charmes Estate Winery 1998 Merlot St. David's Bench Vineyard

Niagara Peninsula VQA $24.95 (453431)
"Chestnuts roasting on an open fire." Can't help but think of the holidays with this wine. Roasted nuts and black cherries dance around the Merlot. The cherries continue the merriment, and the wine leaves some tarry resin on the palate. Wonderfully integrated, this would go well with the roasted turkey dinner or with those roasted chestnuts.

Colio Estate Wines 1999 CEV Merlot Reserve

Niagara Peninsula VQA $21.95 (500447)
It's Halloween for this Merlot as the wine dresses up in an oak costume. With a mask of red ripe fruit, the oat continues to trick and treat its way through the palate. A touch of sweetness with round, soft tannins reveals a deftly made wine. No tricks here—just a fabulous treat.

Gehringer Brothers Estate Winery 1999 Dry Rock Vineyards Merlot

Okanagan Valley VQA $14.95 (559583)
If you're a chocolate bar connoisseur, the one that captures the essence of this wine is Big Turk. Candied chocolate cherries make for a mouth-watering introduction. With a sweet touch the chocolate-cherry flavours carry this light red to the finish. Drinking well now—you could even have this on its own, slightly chilled, or with a salad drizzled with raspberry vinaigrette.

Harbour Estates Winery 2000 Merlot

Niagara Peninsula VQA $25

Although the oak runs the show with this one, the strong presence of black cherries, both in fragrance and flavour, points toward a fabulous wine. Loads of oak give the wine a slightly sweet, vanilla touch on the palate. A full-bodied red that is finely integrated and developed makes this one a keeper. Definitely built to last.

Konzelmann Estate Winery 1999 Merlot Reserve

Niagara Peninsula VQA $10.80 (439281)

This is a bargain hunter's delight. Structured to showcase the fruit, generous notes of cherry cola kick off the show. The fresh fruit—most notably cherries—carries the show through to the credits. The appearance of mint and a dash of sweetness add to the complexity of the wine. For ten bucks, this wine makes you feel rich without breaking the bank.

Mission Hill Estate Winery 1999 Merlot

Okanagan Valley VQA $16.95 (496109)

A lighter version of its reserve twin, this Mission Hill sibling scores with its abundance of raspberry and cassis characteristics. It has good upper body structure with firm tannins and a soft, linger-ing finish. It may not be a reserve, but that hasn't stopped it from trying. If pork is on the menu—this would be a good match.

Southbrook Winery 1999 Merlot

Niagara Peninsula VQA $37.95 (448365)

It's as if Marshal Matt Dillon from *Gunsmoke* opened up a few rounds in the local saloon. Toasty smoke fills the air with some earthy notes kicked up in the process. A touch of gamey sweetness covers the palate with a velvety finish. Pair this one with duck or goose and other wild game.

Tinhorn Creek Vineyards 1998 Merlot

Okanagan Valley VQA $16.95 (530725)

Remember when fondues were the in thing? Shag orange rugs, thick curtains and black faux leather furniture—it was the '70s and disco was king. Well, if you can remember those funky days and fondues were your thing, this wine's like a fondue dipped chocolate cherry. The cherry continues to groove its way through the mouth with oak making an appearance to steal a few moves. Slides back down on the finish in typical Shaft style. Hey, if you are into fondues—this Merlot is a perfect match for your next party.

QUITE GOOD

Calona Vineyards Copper Moon 1999 Merlot

Okanagan Valley VQA $13.95 (580928)

A very berry Merlot. Raspberry rides the flavour wave through to the quick finish. A light and lean Merlot that should be a crowd-pleaser. Think picnic or family reunion.

Calona Vineyards Sandhill 1999 Merlot

Okanagan Valley VQA $15.95 (576751)

A friendly red with lots of fruit—think raspberries and strawberries. Light and lean with fruit continuing to dominate through the finish. Drinking very well now.

Cave Spring Cellars 1998 Merlot

Niagara Peninsula VQA $35 (235051)

Generous notes of mocca coffee fill the glass. Oak and vanilla take over on the palate of this heavily toasted red. The cherry fruit stays tucked away behind the wood, but with a bit of aging or decanting, the fruit should come racing to the front. A wine built for the future, but it will go well now with red meat dishes.

CedarCreek Estates Winery 1998 Merlot

Okanagan Valley VQA $18.95 (408666)

There's not much going on here until the wine hits the taste buds, but once in the mouth, this Merlot unleashes pockets of plum and cherry fruits. The depth of the wine is the key to its success. Extraction of fruit and length of finish make for an ideal wine for the dinner table to accompany pork or veal chops.

Henry of Pelham Family Estate Winery 1999 Merlot

Niagara Peninsula VQA $24.95 (291120)

A welterweight Merlot, the red fruit carries the load. Bing cherries and red currants combine for a one-two punch. A touch of spice rounds out the finish. Should go in the early rounds of a multi-course dinner.

Hernder Estates Winery 1999 Merlot

Niagara Peninsula VQA $16.95 (432567)

Toast with plum jam spread. Oak and red plum rolls through the wine with a bit of cherry bubble gum on the finish. A medium-bodied Merlot that will tackle meaty stews or a spicy chili. A great red for the Grey Cup chili party.

Hester Creek Estate Winery 1999 Merlot

Okanagan Valley VQA $16.85 (467324)

Its leafy fragrance indicates a Merlot from young vines, but the ripe red fruit and cinnamon on the palate take the wine in a different direction. A deft hand with the oak turns this Merlot into a winner with red licorice and lingering tar flavours. Built to be matched with food—wings and Merlot on Saturday night.

Inniskillin Wines 2000 Merlot
Niagara Peninsula VQA $14.95 (323444)
Another youthful Merlot, this one could use a bit of cellar dwelling to give it some character. The fruit remains shy, but after a while in the glass, the fruit starts to express itself. Strawberries are the highlight with ripe tannins carrying the wine.

Jackson-Triggs 1998 Proprietors' Grand Reserve Merlot
Okanagan Valley VQA $24.95 (563197)
This approachable Merlot is smothered in oak. Chocolate notes with sweet cherries and cassis compete for space on the aroma side. Oak wrestles control of the scene on the palate with a medium body assisting in the takeover. A bit too tannic, this wine will do well with a bit of aging.

Peninsula Ridge Estates 1999 Merlot
Niagara Peninsula VQA $24.95
Deep ripe fruit is the hallmark of this wine. Heavy French oak cloaks the fruit, with raisins and plums carrying the torch. Good idea to decant before serving with gamey meat dishes.

Pillitteri Estates Winery 1999 Merlot Reserve
Niagara Peninsula VQA $22.95 (349258)
The fruit seems to have been subdued by the oak. Cedar and tobacco notes dominate the fragrance, then a sweet touch of fruit emerges riding the wave to the finish. The medium-bodied structure and the tannins in front point to this wine aging gracefully.

Willow Heights Winery 2000 Merlot
Niagara Peninsula VQA $25
Wafts of earthiness dominate the nose, but on the palate the fruit explodes with red currants. A hint of sweetness from the oak adds a layer of style to the wine. Rounds out with a slight spicy finish. This one would be at home with pork chops and roasted chicken breasts.

PINOT NOIR

Pinot Noir is the problem child of the vineyard. Call it the Robert Downey Jr. of the wine world because of its puzzling capacity for reaching the highest of highs and plumbing the lowest of lows. It is a total enigma for growers and vintners alike who are desperate to know what makes Pinot tick. Often dubbed the Heartbreak Grape or referred to as winemaking's Holy Grail, this inconsistent grape variety is capable of producing the greatest wines in the world. But consumers have to kiss a lot of frogs before they meet a Pinot worthy of being crowned a prince.

From a winemaking perspective, Pinot demands a greater investment of time and money in the vineyard and at the winery, which is why none of the panel's recommended wines are what you would call cheap. For instance, Pinot Noir benefits from aging in French oak, the most expensive wood barrels on the market.

FOOD PAIRING SUGGESTIONS
Pinot is happy served with most things available at the butcher shop: pork loin or chops, lamb, veal, steak, chicken and game birds including pheasant and duck. It also pairs nicely with salmon, tuna and snapper.

Classic Pinot Noir characteristics are strawberries, cherries, damp soil or compost, and barnyard or horse stables. Newcomers should know that the gamey or rustic aromas are more pleasant than they might seem on first blush. But all Pinot discussions start and end with texture or mouth-feel. Great Pinot is round with a velvety suppleness and a deep penetrating flavour.

The grape's native land is Burgundy in France, which shares some climatic conditions with both Niagara and British Columbia's cool-climate growing regions. Canadian vintners are starting to produce some amazing Pinot Noir, often only in small batches that are snapped up by a cult following. Both regions are working to establish a benchmark from which consistently good wine will flow.

—LC, CR, SP, SS, WS, CW, RW

HIGHLY RECOMMENDED

Burrowing Owl Vineyards 1999 Pinot Noir
Okanagan Valley VQA $18 (556613)
Like Homer's *Odyssey*, this wine is a classic. It is a true reflection of Pinot Noir. The key characters—barnyard, cherries and chocolate—are fully developed. The red fruit takes the lead with a touch of sweetness from the oak providing a strong supporting role. All the characters come together in a complex web of integration as the lingering finish leaves you wanting more. It should age well and become a masterpiece in a few years.

CedarCreek Estate Winery 1998 Pinot Estate Select
Okanagan Valley VQA $24.95 (712125)
CedarCreek's Pinot has a nice plush texture and dollops of slightly sweet fruit. Attractive and approachable, this is a wine to get lost in after dinner as you ponder life, the universe and every-

thing else with that special someone. Trust us, that person has to be special. You don't want to waste this marvel on any Johnny- or Jenny-come-lately.

Inniskillin Okanagan Wines 1998 Pinot Noir Dark Horse Vineyard

Okanagan Valley VQA $19.95 (530840)
A wonderfully rich Pinot with layers of red fruit and oak notes, especially butter and vanilla, this wine is as brooding as Emily Brontë's classic novel *Wuthering Heights*. A penetrating, well-made wine with deep, concentrated flavours that is muted on the nose. But in the mouth, it's as sweeping and stirring as the famous Gothic novel—minus all that tragic doomed love and death, of course.

Inniskillin Wines 1998 Pinot Noir Founders' Reserve

Niagara Peninsula VQA $39.95 (529388)
This was the heavyweight of the tasting. Big, rich and smoky, this bad boy needs some time to mellow out a little. Deeply coloured and extracted, time will soften the mouth-feel until it is supple and velvety. Exotic spices and black cherry flavours merge with some earthy and floral notes in this classically styled Pinot Noir.

Inniskillin Wines 1999 Pinot Noir Montague Estate Vineyard

Niagara Peninsula VQA $29.95 (558148)
Here's a lush, single-vineyard Pinot Noir produced from the warm 1999 vintage. Finely structured, with layers of fruit flavours, soft acidity and ripe tannins combining in a most satisfying manner, this delicious wine is drinking nicely now and will develop over the next four to six years. It compares well with many $50-plus bottles from Burgundy or Oregon and would be superb company for grilled steaks, lamb or stews.

Mission Hill Estate Winery 1999 Pinot Noir Reserve

Okanagan Valley VQA $17.95 (545012)

Good Pinot Noir is often described as being like a velvet glove cast in iron. Its supple texture packs a mighty wallop. This is a good Pinot, so prepare to be rocked by its layers of supple fruit and oak spice. The expressive strawberry and cherry fruit flavours linger longer than a standing-eight count.

RECOMMENDED

Creekside Estate Winery 1999 Pinot Noir

Niagara Peninsula VQA $18.95

Attractive cherry and smoke notes and a tangy, bright acidity are featured in this impressive Pinot that would be perfect with lamb, roast chicken and tuna or salmon steaks. While it's ready to drink now, it has the stuffing to develop for three to five years.

Henry of Pelham Family Estate 1998 Pinot Noir

Niagara Peninsula VQA $24.95 (268391)

Look out! The vanilla, toast and light herbal flavours of this wine come right at you with generous fruit, especially currant and cherry notes that pack a punch. It's a welterweight, but it shows excellent intensity. You can serve it slightly chilled by itself, but it will show better if paired with lamb, mushroom dishes or barbecued dishes.

Hillebrand Estates 1998 Pinot Noir Glenlake Vineyard

Niagara Peninsula VQA $13.95 (980474)

The same way that mild-mannered Dr. Bruce Banner had the Incredible Hulk lurking inside him, this Pinot Noir is enriched by a touch of the beast. A rich core of dried cherry and fig fruit is pumped up by complex leather and rustic earthy notes. The final result is brawny but refined—like Tie Domi dressed in a tux.

Inniskillin Wines 1998 Pinot Noir Reserve
Niagara Peninsula VQA $24.95 (529370)
Are we in Burgundy yet? This benchmark Pinot Noir, with its earthy character and layers of spicy oak, pays allegiance to the well-heeled wines of Burgundy. Sheer luxury for those who enjoy a couple of oak beams in their wine.

Kacaba Vineyards 1999 Pinot Noir
Niagara Peninsula VQA $22.95
Kacaba's ripe and round Pinot features wet earth and dried fruit aromas that suggest taking an autumn walk through the woods while eating trail mix. While on the walk, this wine passes some mushrooms on the palate as well as some ripe wild raspberries and black berries. Just ripe for the picking and the drinking. If you're taking this wine for a walk in the forest, will anyone hear you uncork it?

Quails' Gate Estate Winery 1998 Pinot Noir Family Reserve
Okanagan Valley VQA $35 (560052)
Remember when you were young and all you wanted to do was grow up? That's what this wine is going through. In its youthful stage, it is showing complexity and structure, but it's a bit naïve about how to act in public. Built to age, wait for a couple of years and this one should develop from adolescence into a fine wine. Cherry blossoms dominate the fragrance. Red licorice comes riding in on the palate. Once this wine finds its identity, it will be stellar.

Sumac Ridge Estate Winery 1998 Pinot Noir Private Reserve
Okanagan Valley VQA $15.95 (529370)
Feel like chicken tonight? Spoil yourself by part-nering your mid-week dinner with this lighter, fruit-driven Pinot. The wine's essences of red fruit and toasty aromas make it a natural for roasted chicken or gourmet pizzas.

Sumac Ridge Estate Winery 1999 Pinot Noir
Okanagan Valley VQA $12.95 (392415)
The succulent black cherry fruit and floral aromas are the most beguiling features of this straightforward red wine. It has nice flavours and an attractive mouth-feel that will delight lovers of red wine with loads of juicy fruit.

Tinhorn Creek Vineyards 1999 Pinot Noir
Okanagan Valley VQA $13.95 (530709)
This refreshing wine delivers more cherry and green pepper than animal or earthy funk in the sniff department and plenty of bright acidity in the mouth. The finish is rounded out by a pleasant sweetness, which makes it a perfect partner for fish or fowl—especially pan-fried snapper or salmon.

QUITE GOOD

Château des Charmes Estate Winery 1998 Pinot Noir Estate Bottled
Niagara Peninsula VQA $16.95 (256834)
An attractive wine with perfumey floral aromas mixed with berries and spice. Sweet spice and fruit flavours compete with some bitter notes. A lovely velvety finish saves the day.

Gehringer Brothers Estate Winery 2000 Private Reserve Pinot Noir
Okanagan Valley VQA $13 (430306)
A light, fruit driven Pinot from the Gehringer Brothers. Cherries hold court with wine. From start to finish, the cherry characters carry the wine. Light-bodied with a quick finish, this is the perfect Pinot for Tuesday night pizza and wings.

Inniskillin Wines 1999 Pinot Noir
Niagara Peninsula VQA $13.95 (261099)
This straightforward red wine won't dazzle you with its complexity, but it's off the charts in terms of value. It's chunky, ripe and bright. Serve this with hamburgers, pasta, grilled steaks or chicken or anything that will stand up to a flavourful red.

Jackson-Triggs 1999 Proprietors' Reserve Pinot Noir
Okanagan Valley VQA $14.95 (543868)
Nice clean raspberry aromas with some spice notes on the nose make for an unassuming but approachable Pinot. This would be a popular red to serve at a family reunion or retirement party.

Joseph's Estate Wines 1999 Pinot Noir
Niagara Peninsula VQA $14.95
Light and supple, this fruit-driven Pinot offers essences of red fruit and some floral aromas. This is a crowd-pleasing red that lacks some of the earthy characteristics of classically made Pinot Noir, but is tasty all the same. Try it with barbecued meat or slightly seared fish steaks.

Konzelmann Estate Winery 1998 Pinot Noir Reserve
Niagara Peninsula VQA $19.95 (463141)
A beefy, big-boned Pinot thanks to the wine's extensive slumber in French oak barrels. Rich and complex, this wine has the right stuff to tackle steak or duck.

Larch Hills Winery 1999 Pinot Noir
Salmon Arm, B.C. $13.50 (708685)
Sweet red fruits and some earthy notes add to the charm of this pale but powerful wine. Some floral notes and a short spicy finish add to the drinking pleasure.

Malivoire Wine Co. 1999 Pinot Noir Moira Vineyard

Niagara Peninsula VQA $35.95

Massive oak aromas and animal funk give this wine a fruity fierceness that is more impressive than it is enjoyable at present. An unusually forceful rendition of domestic Pinot, the texture is still soft and silky. Needs time to lurk in the cellar.

Mission Hill Estate Winery 1999 Pinot Noir Bin 99

Okanagan Valley VQA $14.05 (118844)

Well-matched fruit and oak flavours play to a stalemate in this balanced wine that will improve given a year or two of cellaring. Some bottle age will further integrate these attractive elements and make for an extremely fine wine.

Pelee Island Winery 1999 Pinot Noir Reserve Vinedressers Series

Pelee Island, Ont. VQA $13.95 (458521)

Gesundheit! Black pepper and spice aromas tickle the nose, and supple cherry and mouth-watering chokecherry flavours tweak the taste buds in this straight-up wine. It's interesting and exotic.

Quails' Gate Estate Winery 1999 Pinot Noir

Okanagan Valley VQA $16.95 (585760)

An intense wine that offers typical Pinot characteristics such as strawberries and cherries, earth and floral notes. Strong spice essence and wood flavours from extensive barrel aging add to the complexity, making this flavourful wine nice with or without food.

St. Hubertus Estate Winery Oak Bay Vineyard 1999 Pinot Noir Grand Reserve

Okanagan Valley VQA $14.95 (713354)

A pleasant red with chocolate, cherry and vanilla aromas and flavours. Nice texture, nice finish. Drink now.

Stoney Ridge Cellars 1999 Pinot Noir Bench

Niagara Peninsula VQA $12.95 (240903)

Here's a nice value-priced Pinot with good concentration and expressive cherry and raspberry
flavours. Some nice toasty oak notes mellow its
deep fruit flavours.

**Wild Goose Vineyards 1999 Pinot Noir
Hest Vineyard**

Okanagan Valley VQA $13.95 (414711)

Sweet candied fruit aromas carry over to offer
lots and lots of mouth-filling ripe red berry
flavours. This lacks the earthy and complex characteristics of classic Pinot, but it's extremely tasty.
Serve slightly chilled.

Gamay Noir

If you've ever had a Beaujolais red wine, then you've had a Gamay Noir. Made popular by wine-makers of Beaujolais, France, Gamay has become a transition wine for wine enthusiasts. For many novice wine consumers, their appreciation jour-ney starts with light, fruity white wines and evolves to the more complex and full-bodied reds. To get from A to B would be a challenge if it were not for Gamay Noir.

Typically Gamay is built as an expressively fruity, light-bodied red wine with low tannins and high acidity. The approachable style places the wine between the gentle features of whites and the robust features of reds. Since it is usually best enjoyed in its youth, Gamay also gives many wine

FOOD PAIRING SUGGESTIONS
Most Gamay Noirs are built to be consumed now. The fruity, light-bodied styles would go well with hamburgers and tofu burgers. Also grilled chicken and pork and tossed salads would make good companions. Some of the bolder Gamay wines that are being built in Canada could stand up to gourmet pizzas and hot chicken wings.

lovers a chance to try a red wine without having to wait for it to mature for five years or spend the big bucks on an aged red. Some Gamays, however, have been known to age elegantly for more than five to ten years.

The fact that many Gamays are built to be unleashed early and often has given rise to yearly celebrations under the banner of Beaujolais Nouveau or Gamay Nouveau. It's a fitting celebration as the Gamay wine is usually the first red vintage wine every year.

In Canada, Gamay has found a home in Ontario, although there are a couple of producers in British Columbia trying to get it to catch on. Like the Pinot Noir grape, the Gamay grape thrives in the cool climate wine regions of Niagara and the north Okanagan Valley. A vigorous varietal, the grape consistently reaches its full potential year after year. Although not widely produced by wineries in Canada, those that do produce the friendly red wine are beginning to emerge from the shadow cast by the Beaujolais giants. If you want to do a taste test, buy a Gamay from the list below, pair it with a similarly priced Beaujolais and you be the judge of who makes the better Gamay.

—AA, SGB, JI, WS, CW

VINES AWARD

Cave Spring Cellars 1999 Gamay Reserve Estate Bottled

Niagara Peninsula VQA $17.95 (289082)
The sign of a great winemaker is consistency in quality wines from vintage to vintage. Cave Spring's winemaker, Angelo Pavan, has been deftly crafting complex, layered wines since the mid-80s. From vintage to vintage, Pavan rises to the occasion building wines that stand out. His Gamay wines are consistently well-crafted and seamless. The '99 offering continues the tradition

of quality Gamay wines from Cave Spring Cellars. The medium-bodied red opens with a flood of black pepper and black cherry notes. A touch of sweetness from the oak slides the cherry and raspberry flavours across the palate. The real catch for this wine is the extra long finish. It was like starting out on a five-kilometre run and ending up running ten. Although drinking well now, this wine can run for another three to five years without getting tired. Best suited for dishes that focus on the grill—think meaty seafood and pork.

HIGHLY RECOMMENDED

Henry of Pelham Family Estate Winery 1999 Gamay Noir

Niagara Peninsula VQA $11.95 (291112)

A very close second in the Gamay race, this one resembles the Beaujolais approach to Gamay Noir winemaking. This light-bodied red reminded the panel of picking raspberries after a rainfall. The ripe red berries are integrated nicely on the palate while a sprinkle of pepper balances the flavours. As a light-bodied red, this one is ready to be uncorked now.

Lakeview Cellars 1999 Gamay Noir Beamsville Bench

Niagara Peninsula VQA $11.95 (433672)

If this wine could join the Spice Girls, her tag would be Tasty Spice. Loads of black pepper and ground spices spring out of the glass. The spice is joined by a nice blueberry touch on the palate. A soft, round and layered offering finishes with a splash.

Thirteenth Street Winery Sandstone 1998 Gamay Noir

Niagara Peninsula VQA $19.95

Remember when you could drive up to a DQ and get a cherry vanilla ice cream float delivered by a waitress on roller skates? That's what this one does for the memory senses. Loads of fruit and vanilla are layered upon each other with this big, bold offering. Smooth and velvety on the palate— it's a mouth-watering treat. If you have to choose between an ice cream float and this Gamay Noir, pick the wine. Tastes great and doesn't go straight to the hips.

RECOMMENDED

Cave Spring Cellars 2000 Gamay

Niagara Peninsula VQA $11.95 (228569)

The 2000 offering from Cave Spring follows the same lineage as it older '99 sibling. A bit shy, but it should shed its shyness as it ages. Typical notes of pepper and cherries carry over with a touch of spiciness on the palate. Best bet is to give this one some breathing time. Order the pizza, uncork and, when the pizza guy delivers, it should be just about ready.

Château des Charmes Estate Winery 1999 Gamay Noir Droit St. David's Bench Vineyard

Niagara Peninsula VQA $14.95 (057349)

Droit means right in French, and this Gamay is right on. A deft hand with the oak pushed the big black cherries to the front of the wine. A light dash of black pepper with a hint of vanilla sweet-ness makes for a pleasant light-bodied wine. If you like your wings hot, hot, hot, forget the beer. This Gamay will take away a bit of the sting.

Inniskillin Wines 1999 Gamay Noir
Niagara Peninsula VQA $10.95 (082776)
A very berry Gamay. Cherries, raspberries and blackcurrants carry this wine from start to finish. This lightweight red with loads of fruit is an enjoyable wine for sitting around the fire singing camp songs. The more Gamay you have, the more you will think you sound (and look) like Neil Diamond.

QUITE GOOD

Château des Charmes Estate Winery 1999 Gamay Noir
Niagara Peninsula VQA $9.95 (057349)
A leaner offering than its St. David's Bench sibling, this one is crafted to highlight the fruit of the grape. Black cherry and currants make an appearance and fall back on the finish to uncover a touch of spiciness. Pair this wine with medium-spiced chicken wings.

Hawthorne Mountain Vineyards 1998 Gamay Noir
Okanagan Valley VQA $14.95 (440651)
Can I have some wine with this pepper? More fruit on the palate with the pepper taking the back seat to the strawberries and raspberries. Light with a spicy finish. Pairs well with peppercorn steak and baked potatoes or lightly oiled pasta salads.

Hillebrand Estates 1999 Harvest Gamay Noir
Niagara Peninsula VQA $10.25 (291732)
Falters on the start, but, like Donovan Bailey, it picks up some steam through the race and toward the finish. Light cherry flavours dominate with a touch of raspberry making it a fruity red. Comes up a bit short right at the finish line.

Peller Estates 2000 Gamay Noir Founder's Series
Niagara Peninsula VQA $10.75 (342816)
Strawberry, raspberry and a hint of peppermint combine for an interesting, lighthearted red. Gets a bit earthy on the palate, but the bright red fruit comes out for the finish. Serve slightly chilled with some patties and dogs.

St. Hubertus Estate Winery 1999 Gamay Noir Vintner's Reserve
Okanagan Valley VQA $12 (455543)
If you're looking to catch the pie thief, uncork this one and place it by the window. Wafts of cherry come racing out of this wine. The cherries roll through the palate with dashes of sweetness thrown in for good measure. If you're up for a light, lean and fruity red wine, this one is for you.

Other Red Vinifera

FOOD PAIRING SUGGESTIONS
Red meat dishes or spicy stews and chili. For a vegetarian pairing, mushroom-based dishes or stuffed peppers with grilled vegetables.

Patience is indeed a virtue for winemakers and wine lovers looking to see what will become of Syrah/Shiraz in Canada's wine regions. While a lot of young vines are being planted in Ontario and British Columbia, at present there is but a small amount of wine. The early indications are promising, however, with notable wines produced by Inniskillin, Marynissen, Nichol Vineyards and Mission Hill. Only B.C.'s Mission Hill and Nichol Vineyards have produced anything in large enough quantities to dent liquor store shelves.

Syrah and Shiraz are the same grape variety. The difference in names illustrates its country of origin: Syrah for France, where it is the principal red grape of the Rhone Valley, and Shiraz for Australia, where it is the principal red grape for the entire wine industry. In France—a style that Canadian wineries would do better to replicate than chasing Australian jammy reds—Syrah produces earthy, richly fruity, full-bodied red wine with deep blackberry flavor, lush texture and an abundance of rustic charm. Hot-blooded Shiraz from Australia's warm regions (such as McLaren Vale and the Barossa and Hunter Valleys) arguably lack the delicacy and finesse of their French cousins. These wines, however, are wildly popular with consumers the world over, which obviously is leading Canadian producers to favour using this moniker. The problem is that, barring an alarming increase in global warming, no Canadian vineyard is ever going to bake under the same hot sun that pumps up Aussie Shiraz.

—RD, TK, WS, JW, CW

RECOMMENDED

Joseph's Estate Wines 1999 Petite Sirah Reserve

Niagara Peninsula VQA $24.95

An interesting and approachable wine, there's nothing petite about this big red that offers a most evocative fresh pepper aroma. Pepper dominates the flavour profile as well, liberally seasoning the subtle red and black fruit flavours. Deep and persistent, this wine is best enjoyed in the next year or two. Serve with steak and grilled vegetables.

Mission Hill Estate Winery 1999 Shiraz

Okanagan Valley VQA $17.95 (585778)

An explosion of ripe fruit seasoned with pepper and buttery oak, Mission Hill has got one foot in the New World, the other in the Old World. The wine's aromas suggest an Australian fruit bomb, but the flavours are earthy and pepper à la Rhone. Layers of dense fruit and spicy vanilla refresh the palate, while the concentrated black fruit flavours linger on the long finish.

Nichol Vineyard 1998 Syrah Unfiltered
Okanagan Valley $21.90 (700856)

A rustic Rhone-like red wine with peppery black cherry and gamey flavours and aromas, this is serious wine—perhaps a bit austere. It is dry and lean with a nice intense mouth-feel. Earthy notes combine with tart cherry and black pepper flavours on the lingering finish.

Red Hybrids

BACO NOIR

FOOD PAIRING SUGGESTIONS: Being quintessentially Canadian, Baco Noir goes well with caribou, venison, duck and back bacon over the grill at the cottage.

If Bob and Doug MacKenzie were wine drinkers, they would probably uncork a few bottles of Baco Noir while watching *Hockey Night in Canada*. It's a hearty hybrid that grows very well in Canada's cooler wine regions. Although not widely planted in British Columbia, a few producers in Ontario have taken a liking to the robust red and turned it into a cult favourite. It's like the John Candy of the wine world—big, boisterous, unpretentious and fun to be around.

—SGB, TK, WS, CW

VINES AWARD

Henry of Pelham Family Estate 1999 Baco Noir Reserve
Ontario VQA $21.95 (461699)

The reigning king of Baco Noir is Henry of Pelham. Year after year, Henry of Pelham manages to produce a wonderfully tasty Baco. It's almost a given that when you unleash a Baco from HOP, you're going to get a wine that will stain your tongue a deep purple and leave your taste buds wanting more. Dark chocolate with hints of tobacco and plum increase in intensity as the wine coats the palate. Rich and full of complexity, this Baco has a long, lingering finish. If you're the hunting type, take a couple of bottles of this Baco to the lodge.

HIGHLY RECOMMENDED

Henry of Pelham Family Estate 1999 Baco Noir
Ontario VQA $11.95 (270926)
You can fly economy but still feel like a first-class traveller with HOP's less expensive '99 Baco. It has many of the elements of its more expensive twin, it's just a little lighter. A yummy wine with pepper and figs taking the lead role with a touch of oak and red berries finishing it off. Loads of flavour will make it a dinner table favourite when enjoying fresh game meats.

Lakeview Cellars 1999 Baco Noir
Ontario VQA $9.95 (307181)
If you really like chocolate, unleash this gem and wait for those intense, dark, rich aromas. The chocolate carries this wonderful red through to the end with a nice lingering finish. Forget the box of chocolates on Valentine's Day; get your special someone a bottle of this and let the evening unfold.

Thomas & Vaughan Vintners 1999 Baco Noir
Ontario VQA $12.95
Imagine picking plums in an orchard surrounded by lilacs while enjoying a cup of tea. If you can picture that, you've got a good imagination—and you've got a good idea what to expect from this wine. Full-bodied and robust, there's a hint of tobacco on the palate that takes the wine home.

RECOMMENDED

Stoney Ridge Cellars 1999 Baco Noir Old Vines
Ontario VQA $11.95 (240895)

How old do you have to be before you're called old? In vine years, if you've been in the ground for more than twenty years, you get labelled "old." If that were the case with humans, there would be a lot fewer young punks hanging around listening to all that loud noise. On the other hand, there would be a lot more people wearing white pants pulled up above the waist complaining about the government and the weather. Either way, Stoney Ridge's Old Vines Baco has a rich, plummy goodness to it. With floral and plum notes mixing it up, this Baco rides to the finish with some soft, supple tannins. If you're celebrating a long weekend with a barbecue, this oldster could help spin a few "remember when" stories.

Thomas & Vaughan Vintners 2000 Baco Noir
Ontario VQA $12.95

Different from the '99 offering from T&V, this one has loads of pepper and spice characteristics. A little leaner, with plums coming out from behind the pepper on the palate, this wine would be the perfect match for grilled steak or hamburgers.

QUITE GOOD

Harrow Estates 1999 Baco Noir
Ontario VQA $8.95 (559179)

Have you ever wondered what wine would go well with peanut butter and jam sandwiches? This is the sort of question that keeps wine writers up nights. And we think we've found the answer. The red fruit flavours are packaged into this Baco like freshly canned jam. Best enjoyed now and slightly chilled.

Pelee Island Winery 2000 Baco Noir
Ontario VQA $8.95 (485128)

A youthful Baco, this one could use a bit of time in the decanter to open up some of its expressive notes of chocolate and plums. The fruit comes out to play on the palate, but the finish leaves a bit of a tart aftertaste. Best suited beside a cheese platter with loads of old smoked cheeses.

Reif Estate Winery 2000 Baco Noir
Ontario VQA $10.95 (233106)

This is a kinder, gentler Baco with hints of chocolate and floral notes. Its soft, supple texture makes for an enjoyable wine on the back patio with Italian sausages on the grill.

MARÉCHAL FOCH

A French hybrid, Maréchal Foch sounds like the name of a French-Canadian hockey player: "Maréchal Foch, Montreal's leading scorer, rushes down the left wing. He shoots, he ..." you get the idea. This is a winter-hardy vine, and winemakers can count on the grapes reaching their full potential year after year. Although not widely popular with wine aficionados, it has its loyal followers. There are only a handful of producers in British Columbia and Ontario making Maréchal Foch, but wineries in Quebec have planted acre upon acre of the varietal.

—SGB, TK, WS, CW

FOOD PAIRING SUGGESTIONS
Mushroom-based dishes and gamey meats such as venison, rabbit and duck.

HIGHLY RECOMMENDED

Lakeview Cellars 1998 Maréchal Foch
Ontario VQA $9.95 (514752)

Memories of sitting in a dark theatre watching *Star Wars* with a bucket of popcorn and a cherry cola. The cola joins forces with vanilla as the wine slices and dices its way through the mouth. As it comes to a close, it lingers around before heading off for a planet far, far away. Looking forward to the sequel.

Malivoire Wine Co. 1999 Old Vines Foch
Ontario VQA $18.95 (551036)

Although Foch is a New World wine, Malivoire's offering illustrates how a Burgundian winemaker would make a Foch. Full of earthy goodness with a hint of barnyard, this wine was built to last. Buttery characteristics soften the palate with a deft stick handling of the oak. A touch of sweetness rolls the wine home for a full finish. Best enjoyed with gamey meats or grilled mushrooms. This is definitely a benchmark Maréchal Foch. It would also go well with cigars and a gentleman's game of poker.

Thomas & Vaughan Vintners 1999 Maréchal Foch Old Vine
Ontario VQA $12.95

Big, bold and plummy is the best way to describe this Foch. It leaves a nice purple stain on the teeth and lingers around for a while on the finish. Probably not the best bet for drinking on a first date—unless you want to have a smile like Austin Powers'.

RECOMMENDED

Hernder Estate Wines 1999 Foch
Ontario VQA $8.95 (557371)

This Foch stumbled into some American oak and decided to stay. The oak contact has developed a vanilla fragrance in the wine. The sweet touch of the oak gives it a nice supple mouth-feel with a flashy finish.

Quails' Gate Estate Winery 1999 Old Vines Foch Limited Release

Okanagan Valley VQA $19.95 (411348)

If you're a fan of *This Old House*, you'll like this oaky offering. This Old Foch sat in some new American oak for a while. Loads of toasty vanilla coat the fruit with plums adding some colour to the walls. Open the windows and let this one air out if you're not a new oak fan. Could be a nice companion to smoked salmon or steak.

QUITE GOOD

D'Angelo Estate 1999 Old Vines Foch Reserve

Ontario VQA $15 (547737)

California raisins make an appearance once you get a whiff of this wine. The raisins continue to dance and sing their way through to the finish of this medium-bodied Foch. Not overtly complex but would hold up well with stews.

Magnotta Winery 1999 Maréchal Foch

Ontario VQA $6.65

Notes of baked cherry pie offer an enticing entry. The flavours in the mouth include something that resembles a raspberry that has dropped to the earth. A streak of acidity breaks up the flavour profile, but a medium finish brings the raspberry and plum flavours crashing back. Ideal for the patio with burgers and hot dogs.

St. Hubertus Estate Winery Oak Bay Vineyard 1999 Maréchal Foch Grand Reserve

Okanagan Valley VQA $15 (462507)

Remember your first dance. She had the fragrance of cherry lip gloss and vanilla body wash. The air was filled with buttery popcorn. That's this wine. A light, lean Foch with tasty cola and vanilla flavours gliding effortlessly over the palate. If only that had been the case with your awkward dancing moves.

DESSERT WINE

ICEWINE

Icewine. The sweet nectar of the gods. The golden honey of wine. Whatever you want to call it, Icewine is sweet, seductive and expensive. It has become Canada's most well-known wine export, and with the recent European Union's decision to allow Canadian Icewine to be imported into the EU, its popularity will only continue to grow.

It's a rare and elegant wine unlike any other, made from frozen grapes that have been left on the vine for late harvest, usually in December and January. According to Canadian Icewine standards set by the VQA, Icewine grapes can be harvested only after the temperature reaches -8°C or colder. The grapes are pressed immediately while still frozen. The yield for such grapes is only 75 to 100 litres of intensely flavoured juice per tonne of grapes. To craft an exquisite Icewine,

FOOD PAIRING SUGGESTIONS
Some people serve Icewine with foie gras, but it is best enjoyed after dinner. Instead of thigh-enhancing desserts, opt for a glass of slightly chilled Icewine.

the winemaker must balance the highly concentrated sugar levels with the low acidity of the juice. An Icewine without balanced acidity is pancake syrup. Well-made vintages are sweet but never cloying.

Through a number of international wine competitions, including the prestigious VinExpo in France and VinItaly in Italy, Canadian Icewine has helped place Canadian wines on the world stage. The two most popular grapes for Canadian Icewine are Riesling and Vidal. In Ontario, the hardy Vidal grape was the first to be successfully turned into Icewine. Its thick skin makes it ideal for allowing the grape juice to freeze without splitting open and losing valuable liquid. Although Vidal is not as abundant in British Columbia, Riesling has become a popular alternative in that province's Icewine arena. In both Ontario and British Columbia, many producers are crafting dazzling Riesling Icewines.

As the popularity of Icewine grows around the world, winemakers are continuing to experiment with different varieties in hopes of creating more rare and exotic vintages. Icewines made from Gewürztraminer, Pinot Gris, Pinot Blanc, Ehrenfelser and red viniferas like Cabernet Franc, Pinot Noir and Merlot all made appearances in our exhaustive tasting. One quick note: Unless otherwise specified, the prices quoted are for the traditional 375 mL bottle.

—LB, WH, WS, CW, BY

Vidal Icewine

VINES AWARD

Reif Estate Winery 1999 Vidal Icewine
Niagara Peninsula VQA $46.95 (544775)
Like Fred Astaire and Ginger Rogers' dazzling
dance numbers in *Shall We Dance?* Reif's Vidal
Icewine is a perfect pairing of flavour and substance. A sequence of peaches, apricots and
pears bursts from this luscious offering. The
dance of perfection continues on the palate,
where the peaches and apricots join forces. The
finely balanced foundation of acids and sugars
guides the flavours through to an elegantly
extended finish. A golden masterpiece.

HIGHLY RECOMMENDED

Château des Charmes Estate Winery 1998 Vidal Icewine
Niagara Peninsula VQA $45 (413732)
The perfect match for listening to Rufus
Wainwright's 2001 release *Poses.* Floral and fruity
fragrances of honeysuckle, chamomile, honey
and apricots seduce you. A wonderful, silky
mouth-feel with luscious flavours of honey and
apricots caress the palate, and the finish leaves
you wanting more. A touch on the sweet side,
but a layer of acid balances it out in the end.

Pillitteri Estate Winery 1999 Vidal Icewine
Niagara Peninsula VQA $49.95 (370007)
Pillitteri's offering mesmerizes the senses with
its beauty. Flavours of honey, chamomile and
peaches gently tug at the taste buds. Once
inside, the fruit fills the mouth and the wine
caresses the palate, sweetness slipping in and
out between the layers of crisp acidity. The
lingering finish ends with a sweet stroke.

Royal DeMaria Winery 1999 Vidal Icewine

Niagara Peninsula VQA $42.95

Tagged as Canada's Icewine specialists, Royal DeMaria has put its money where its wine is with its Vidal offering. Wafts of chamomile and honey tickle the nose with flavours of chamomile carrying over onto the palate. One can see the close attention to detail in the winemaking process here; design and structure are finely integrated. This creates the ideal Icewine—one that doesn't smack you in the face with its sweetness.

Strewn Wines 1999 Vidal Icewine

Niagara Peninsula VQA $45 (467738)

When a winemaker hits a home run with an Icewine, you're in for a special treat. Strewn's '99 offering went over the left field wall. A whopper with typical apricot, peach and honey characteristics swelling over to the palate. With a sweet swing, the acidity and alcohol slice through, creating an Icewine that is not too cloying and has a nice finish. Call this one Mr. October.

RECOMMENDED

Hillebrand Estates 1998 Showcase Vidal Icewine Barrel Fermented

Niagara Peninsula VQA $60 (980144)

Looking for a winter holiday wine? This one would do just fine. For a slightly different style, Hillebrand has oak-aged this winter treat. Pleasant notes of honey, chamomile and dried apricot dance through the air. On the palate, it borders on cloying, but it balances itself out with a lingering finish.

Lakeview Cellars 1999 Vidal Icewine

Niagara Peninsula VQA $18.95/200 mL (522672)
Here's a wine for caramel lovers. It has the classic apricot and peaches of a Vidal Icewine with an added profile of caramel toffee. The fruit and toffee are accented by a load of weight on the palate. A sweet streak runs through the body capping the wine off with a heightened sweet kick at the end.

Southbrook Winery 1999 Vidal Icewine

Niagara Peninsula VQA $29.95 (526634)
While a little shy at first, the more time this wine spends mingling in the glass, the more it opens up. Once comfortable with its surroundings, it unleashes its fresh tropical fruits. The big surprise is the palate. Unlike the shy nose, the body of the wine is built like a heavyweight fighter. Big and bold layers of fruit take the wine home making friends with everyone. Notably bigger than most of the other offerings, this one will age very well.

Stonechurch Vineyards 1996 Vidal Icewine

Niagara Peninsula VQA $44.95 (477596)
For a good example of how well Icewine ages, check out this five-year-old. Much of the fruit has been replaced with notes of roasted hazelnuts, caramel, toffee and honey. On the palate, the caramel and toffee swirl through the wine leading to a big, lingering finish.

Stoney Ridge Cellars 1999 Vidal Icewine

Niagara Peninsula VQA $39.95 (314682)
"On Golden Pond" would be an ideal name for this Icewine. Its rich, deep, golden brown colour gives way to an interesting fragrance of peppermint and roasted nuts. Soft caramel flavours blanket the palate. Well built and balanced.

QUITE GOOD

Konzelmann Estates Winery 1998 Vidal Icewine

Niagara Peninsula VQA $42.95 (476192)

If you're not one to venture to the sweet side of Icewine enjoyment, Konzelmann's '98 offering celebrates its lighter side. Built along the lines of a select late harvest, this wine's highlights include lean apricot and honey on the nose. A nice, crisp acidity carries the light fruit flavours without pushing too hard on the finish.

Reif Estate Winery 1998 Vidal Icewine

Niagara Peninsula VQA $46.95 (544775)

This would be the ideal drink for Detective Steve McGarrett and Detective Kono of *Hawaii Five-0*. They could have reminisced about pineapples and grass skirts. Reif's '98 offering is on the lighter side of a typical Icewine. It's not overtly sweet, making it even more enjoyable after spending some time on ice.

Thirty Bench Winery 1998 Vidal Icewine

Niagara Peninsula VQA $41.95 (557298)

Aromas of caramel, toffee and coffee bean swing the memory back to lazy afternoons in Starbucks. The flavours drift toward the coffee bean profile complete with a slight bitterness. No loitering allowed as the finish exits stage left.

Vineland Estates 1998 Vidal Icewine

Niagara Peninsula VQA $42

If you're looking for an Icewine that will appeal to a wide range of guests, this delicately crafted one would be perfect. Soft touches of honey and lychee gently wash through the wine without a glimpse of cloying sweetness. A lovely lingering finish caps this elegant offering.

Willow Heights Winery 1999 Vidal Icewine
Niagara Peninsula VQA $36.95 (580134)
This is one big, thick and juicy wine. Huge notes of peaches and honey offer a one-two punch to the nose. On the palate, the punches come fast and furious with blow after blow of rich, fruit flavours. The finish takes one last swing before going down for the ten count.

Riesling Icewine

VINES AWARD

Vineland Estates 1998 Riesling Icewine
Niagara Peninsula VQA $65
If there were an Olympic medal for Icewine, Vineland's Riesling Icewine would be on the podium. With high marks for fragrance, flavour and finesse, the wine is flawless. Delicate aromas of lemon, lime and pineapple combine for a powerful entry. These are followed by finely balanced layers of fruit, acid and alcohol creating an intense and lush presence on the palate. The lingering finish nails the performance. A perfect ten across the board—no need for a drug test on this one.

HIGHLY RECOMMENDED

Henry of Pelham Family Estate Winery 1999 Riesling Icewine
Niagara Peninsula VQA $54.95 (430561)
If Laura Secord had passed Henry of Pelham on her way to warn the Redcoats of an American invasion, she may not have made it if this wine had been around. Henry of Pelham's '99 offering opens with lovely citrus and floral fragrances. A wash of fresh fruit covers the palate with a mouth-feel that is sweet but not too over-powering. A streaking finish wraps up the ride.

Inniskillin Okanagan Wines 1999 Riesling Icewine Dark Horse Vineyard

Okanagan Valley $59.95 (558445)

Speaking of dark horses, this one almost took top honours. Intriguing notes of beeswax, vanilla, pineapple and pear cascade from the glass. A bright, crisp acidity accents the fruit with expressive pear and pineapple taking the lead. The finish leaves you yearning for more.

Jackson-Triggs 1999 Proprietors' Grand Reserve Riesling Icewine

Okanagan Valley VQA $52.95 (572057)

You can either pop a tropical flavoured Jolly Rancher into your mouth or unleash this Icewine. With J-T's offering, you get tropical fruit flavours of lemon, pineapple and chamomile. A lemon zing races through the wine from start to finish, capping it off with a crisp, refreshing finish.

Peller Estates 1999 Andrew Peller Signature Series Riesling Icewine

Niagara Peninsula VQA $60 (981175)

This is bear-friendly wine; the marmalade and beeswax fragrances would drive Pooh wild. Toasty notes enhance the fruit but don't interfere with their flavours. A citrus hint buzzes around with a slight sweet kick in the back. Overall, the wine is balanced with a lingering tropical finish. Don't worry Pooh, there's enough for all your friends.

RECOMMENDED

Château des Charmes Estate Winery 1999 Estate Bottled Riesling Icewine

Niagara Peninsula VQA $59.95

The lemon and grapefruit wait for the right moment to move in on the crooks. The sign is given and as lemon and grapefruit climb out of the car, wafts of petrol notes fill the air. Once inside the joint, the fruity duo takes on the acid and sugar. A quick exchange of fire ends with the lemon knocking both off. Never mess with fruit cops, they always get their man. Nice work.

Cave Spring Cellars 1998 Riesling Icewine

Niagara Peninsula VQA $59.95 (447441)

Deep in the cellars of Cave Spring lurks a ghost. Legend has it that late at night, the ghost can be seen attempting to cut through vats of Icewine with an old chainsaw while eating lemons. The '98 vintage has spooky fragrances of citrus and petrol. On the palate, it has a rich and velvety mouth-feel with the eerie appearance of lemon. Before you know it, it's gone. Maybe it's time to call Mulder and Scully.

Inniskillin Okanagan Wines 1998 Riesling Icewine

Okanagan Valley VQA $59.95 (530857)

Get out the Hawaiian shirts. Pleasant aromas of tropical fruit, including lovely pineapple and passion fruit notes, take the mind away from the dreary winters of Canada. The tropical flavours shine through to the long, lingering finish. Don't forget the sunscreen.

Malivoire Wine Co. 1999 Riesling Icewine
Niagara Peninsula VQA $35.95/275 mL
Malivoire's debut vintage Icewine thrills with its special effects of delicious tropical fruit and sponge candy notes. The elements of this lush and intense single-vineyard Icewine are finely integrated with lemon and pineapple carrying through the weight of the wine. The crisp, brisk finish leaves the palate wanting a few more thrills.

Paradise Ranch Wines 2000 Riesling Icewine
Okanagan Valley VQA $49.95 (587139)
Paradise Ranch specializes in the production of Icewine and has rounded up some fine fruit for its Riesling edition. Lemon, lime and a hint of pineapple are herded onto the plains of the palate. A good backbone with a crisp acidity keeps this offering out of trouble.

QUITE GOOD

Harbour Estates Winery 1999 Riesling Icewine
Niagara Peninsula VQA $54.95
This debut vintage from a new Jordan winery, Harbour Estates, features a pleasing floral nose and pleasantly sweet mouth-feel. Bright pineapple flavour and aroma add to the enjoyment. Two chairs, one deck, a sunset and this one on ice—life doesn't get any better.

Hernder Estate Wines 1999 Riesling Icewine
Niagara Peninsula VQA $29.95 (563304)
A tropical storm ripped through this wine with pineapple, lemons and honeydew melon whirling around out of control. The epicentre of the storm localizes on the palate with pineapple crashing around. A stream of acidity merges with a slightly cloying mouth-feel as the storm passes through to the finish. Tropical storm chasers beware.

Inniskillin Wines 1998 Riesling Icewine
Niagara Peninsula VQA $69.95 (534412)
Citrus combines with some interesting earthy
flavours in this big-bodied Icewine, which is rich,
yet balanced.

**Konzelmann Estate Winery 1998 Matthias
Riesling Icewine**
Niagara Peninsula VQA $53.95 (542399)
A fruit forward offering with expressive notes of
zesty lime and lemon. Although slightly high on
the acidity scale, the crisp, clean mouth-feel
offers a refreshing option for Icewine fans who
believe less sweet is better.

Pillitteri Estate Winery 1999 Riesling Icewine
Niagara Peninsula VQA $29.95/200 mL (435727)
Lovers of mangoes and peaches should check
this one out. Lovely peach and dried mango
flavours make for a nicely styled vintage. Its
honeyed mouth-feel is rich and a tad sweet
but has tons of fruit.

**Quails' Gate Estate Winery 1998 Riesling
Icewine**
Okanagan Valley VQA $54.95 (539239)
Pronounced fruit, especially pineapple, and
roasted marshmallow aromas combine with a
sweet but balanced mouth-feel in this lively,
refreshing Icewine. It finishes with a clean
sweep of acidity.

Southbrook Winery 1998 Riesling Icewine
Niagara Peninsula VQA $29.95/200 mL (559229)
This big, bold Icewine missed the elevator to the
fruit department. Very subtle citrus and roasted
nut aromas tiptoe through the wine, but an
above-average mouth-feel makes for a pleasant,
liquid-gold treat.

Strewn Wines 1999 Riesling Icewine

Niagara Peninsula VQA $58.95 (554394)

Caramel and honeyed aromas swirl in the glass of this vintage, which is harmonious but slightly bitter on the palate. Excellent mouth-feel and a good finish make for a pleasant Icewine.

Thirty Bench Winery 1998 Riesling Icewine

Niagara Peninsula VQA $54.90 (412932)

Thirty Bench's '98 vintage is a harmonious wine with delicious honey and caramel notes. Quite sweet on the palate, but with acidity to match, it offers caramel, some petrol flavours and a good finish.

Other Icewines

VINES AWARD

Calona Vineyards 1999 Pinot Noir Icewine

Okanagan Valley VQA $140

A rare species in the Icewine kingdom, this is the first commercially available Pinot Noir Icewine from Calona Vineyards and it's absolutely divine. With winemakers continuing to experiment with red vinifera Icewines, Pinot Noir has been given little chance of success due to its fickle nature and thin skin—until now. From the bright red colour through to the expressive red berry characteristics, this Icewine is amazing. On the palate, a fresh, crisp acidity keeps the sugar at bay as cherry and red currant flavours wash over the palate. It's rounded out by a long, flavourful finish that truly caps this special wine.

HIGHLY RECOMMENDED

Jackson-Triggs 1999 Gewürztraminer Icewine
Niagara Peninsula VQA $59.95 (569293)

When a winemaker can craft a Gewürztraminer Icewine with its trademark aromatics and crisp acidity, then wrap a blanket of sweetness around it, you're in for a special treat. The offering from Jackson-Triggs starts with a sweet fragrance of rose petal and subtle notes of ripe lychee fruit. The fruit carries on to the palate with a streak of acidity that counters the sugar, leaving the wine crisp and full of flavour.

Inniskillin Wines 1999 Cabernet Franc Icewine
Niagara Peninsula VQA $89.95 (558270)

Red Icewine is a relatively new phenomenon, and Inniskillin has been leading the way in experimenting with new styles. The '99 Cabernet Franc leans on the sweet side of the spectrum, but sweet cherry jam and raspberry flavours capture the typical characteristics of Cabernet Franc. This truly is romance in a bottle.

Paradise Ranch Wines 2000 Merlot Icewine
Okanagan Valley VQA $58.95 (587147)

Here's another red wonder. The fruit from this Merlot shines through with good concentration. Red currants and cranberry flavours are like a beacon of light inside the depths of acidity and sugar. Although a touch too sweet on the palate, the crisp finish and bright fruit balance it out. This is Merlot magic with a twist.

RECOMMENDED

Pillitteri Estates Winery 1999 Gewürztraminer Icewine

Niagara Peninsula VQA $49.95 (349092)

This G-wine Icewine has serious attitude. A shell of nutty goodness covers hints of rose petal and honey. Almond and tangerine tango on the palate with a spicy, hot finish that lingers around for a while. Higher on the acidity scale, this is definitely not a flabby Icewine. It flexes its muscles from start to finish.

Stoney Ridge Cellars 1999 Barrel-Fermented Gewürztraminer Icewine

Niagara Peninsula VQA $95

Forget about the mocha cappuccino fix, reach for this lovely, luscious vintage with its creamy mouth-feel that offers loads of mocha and butterscotch flavours. Why drink decaf when you can enjoy a chilled glass of this beauty?

Sumac Ridge Estate Winery 1998 Pinot Blanc Icewine

Okanagan Valley VQA $49.95 (453936)

A golden treat of ripe yellow delicious apples with pears and a hint of vanilla. Finely balanced between sugar and acidity, flavours of honey and pear congregate on the palate, lingering just long enough to leave you yearning for more.

QUITE GOOD

Hernder Estates Wines 1999 Pinot Gris Icewine

Niagara Peninsula VQA $90 (563312)

A pronounced lavender aroma makes this a very interesting Icewine. Pinot Gris is not typically known as an Icewine grape, but it has managed to produce a beautifully aromatic and sweet wine.

Paradise Ranch Wines 2000 Chardonnay Icewine

Okanagan Valley VQA $58.95 (587006)
Chardonnay is another grape not widely produced as Icewine. Paradise Ranch's Chard Icewine has attractive banana and brown-sugar-baked-pear aromas. Banana and vanilla lightly glide across the palate. Although a little on the lean side, the expressive flavours make it enjoyable as a quick fix after a long day at the office.

Royal DeMaria Wines 1999 Pinot Gris Icewine

Niagara Peninsula VQA $79.95
This Pinot Gris Icewine is softer than expected and its mouth-feel is leaner than most Icewines. However, this elegant offering is a wonderful change of pace from Vidal and Riesling vintages.

LATE HARVEST WINES

When it comes to Canadian dessert wines, Icewine generally hogs all the attention. Why not? It's got a dramatic storyline. Left behind in the vineyard to face an uncertain future, confined to a mesh prison, defenceless against the peril of birds and the wintery blasts of inclement weather, the grapes are rescued and pressed under the frozen dark of night to produce one of the world's finest wines.

However, that epic tale comes at a price. The late harvest wines produced in Ontario and British Columbia have no such history. But does that mean we should deny them the love and attention they so richly deserve? We think not.

As Canadian vintners continue to experiment with and improve their production of Icewine, that level of knowledge asserts itself with the wineries'

FOOD PAIRING SUGGESTIONS
Keep in mind, these wines can be served instead of dessert, as an aperitif or in between courses during a formal dinner. We suggest pairing them with creamy cheeses and a dish of nuts or fresh fruit desserts that are less sweet than the wine. Salty meats, especially ham or prosciutto, or foie gras would also be a good match for these sweet wines.

late harvest wines, which can range in sugar levels from medium-sweet sippers to baby Icewines (in the case of Special Select Late Harvest wines).

In general, the results of our panel tasting were quite eye-opening—as were the prices. Wineries are turning late harvest Riesling and Vidal into sumptuous wines that are perfectly suited to adding some elegance to your next dinner party. The lighter-bodied style results in a more food-friendly beverage. They can make a big impression without taxing your budget as much as Icewines, which is something to consider if you took a beating backing the wrong dot-com.

Riesling and Vidal aren't the only grape varieties allowed to stay out late in the vineyards. There were also a few late harvest Gewürztraminer, Chardonnay, Ehrenfelser and Ortega vintages that ranked high on our score cards.

—LB, WH, WS, CW

VINES AWARD

Thirty Bench Winery 1999 Special Select Late Harvest Riesling
Niagara Peninsula VQA $24.95
Seductive and powerful, like that scene in *To Have and Have Not* when Lauren Bacall tells Humphrey Bogart how to whistle. This fabulous late harvest wine presents a lovely mouth-feel and bright notes of honey, citrus and peach. A textbook sweet wine, it is full and rich, but finely balanced with a lively acidity that keeps the sweetness in check. This pleasurable wine, which benefited from the concentrating effect of botrytis (a naturally occurring vineyard fungus that concentrates the grape sugars and adds a honey flavour to the wine), has the right stuff to cellar for the next four to six years, perhaps longer. More than a dessert wine, this is dessert.

HIGHLY RECOMMENDED

Cave Spring Cellars 2000 Late Harvest Riesling Indian Summer

Niagara Peninsula VQA $21.95 (415901)

This is a very social late harvest wine. It blends in with the food and fun at your dinner table, adding another layer of sophistication to your perfect night at home. A beautifully balanced wine, this Riesling-based sweetie is medium-bodied with a plush mouth-feel enhanced by sweet citrus flavours and lively acidity. It offers strong varietal character, especially aromas of citrus, a hint of petrol and chamomile, and a long lingering, slightly nutty finish.

Hawthorne Mountain Vineyards 1999 Late Harvest Ehrenfelser

Okanagan Valley VQA $19.95 (567057)

A unique and approachable late harvest, the only thing difficult about this sweet Ehrenfelser is the spelling of its name. Fragrant aromas of lanolin, rose perfume and beeswax and an attractive fleshy-fruit mouth-feel stand out in this delicious wine. Deep and concentrated, this delivers an intense burst of flavour that is sealed with a lingering candied citrus kiss.

Thirteenth Street Winery 1998 Sandstone Select Late Harvest Riesling

Niagara Peninsula VQA $17.50

"Pretty lady!" Like Jerry Lewis in *The Nutty Professor*, this serious wine is slightly fruity and extremely nutty. Unlike Lewis, however, it's never, ever annoying. A wonderful late harvest offering, this immaculate wine delivers peach, apricot and chamomile aromas with some interesting and complex notes of nuts and toffee. Very fine, with well-woven sweetness and acidity, it will develop over the next four years. Excellent balance, length and value for the price. The French would love it.

LATE HARVEST WINES

RECOMMENDED

Cilento Wines 1999 Special Select Late Harvest Riesling

Ontario VQA $19.95 (510313)

Lovely aromatics, generous fruit on the nose (passion fruit and kiwi), a light mouth-feel that features lively acidity and a touch of bitterness make for an elegant wine. Balanced with a long finish, this is fabulous served as an aperitif or as dessert with creamy cheeses and pâtés. Your guests will no doubt be impressed by your extreme good taste. At this price, so will your accountant.

Crown Bench Estates 1999 Livia's Gold Sweet Chardonnay Estate Bottled

Niagara Peninsula VQA $24.95

The perfumed and almost herbaceous aromatics of this wine make it quite usual but extremely pleasant. The palate is full, very sweet and power-ful with balanced acidity. A great talking point to conclude a festive winter meal. Some people might enjoy trifle and tea, but other guests will want to contemplate life, staring at the dancing flames in the fireplace and sipping this rich nectar.

Inniskillin Wines 1999 Special Select Late Harvest Riesling

Niagara Peninsula VQA $34.95 (560599)

Here's a bouncing baby late Riesling that features subtle aromas of lime, citrus and some mineral notes. On the palate it is medium-bodied and sweet with a lush mouth-feel and a resonating citrus-tinged finish. The sweetness of this wine would match well with salty foods, such as Roquefort or prosciutto and melon.

St. Hubertus Estate Winery 1998 Vintner's Reserve Summer Symphony

Okanagan Valley VQA $9.95 (436782)

A blend of late harvest Riesling and Pinot Blanc, this delicious and value-priced wine features pronounced aromas of perfume and tropical fruits along with slightly earthy (almost cheese-like) notes. The perfume carries through to the palate of this full-bodied vintage that is warm, fruity and balanced.

QUITE GOOD

Château des Charmes Estate Winery 1997 Late Harvest Sauvignon Blanc Barrel Fermented St. David's Bench Vineyard

Niagara Peninsula VQA $24.95 (582346)

Honey and toffee-like aromas intermingle with toasted bread and herbaceous notes in this sweet wine. On the palate, flavours of flowery lemon blossom and dried apricot emerge. A zesty acidity cuts through the rich and full texture.

Château des Charmes Estate Winery 1998 Estate Bottled Late Harvest Riesling

Niagara Peninsula VQA $19.95 (432930)

Intense honey, peach and petrol aromas storm out of the glass. The petrol notes dominate on the palate, with the ripe peach and citrus flavours emerging on the long, expressive finish. Rich and succulent, this vintage is sweet but balanced with lively acidity.

Colio Estate Wines 1998 Select Late Harvest Riesling

Lake Erie North Shore VQA $17.95 (532499)

Golden in colour, medium intensity on the nose offering minerals, petrol and grapefruit peel. The palate is sweet, syrupy, balanced and delicious. The finish is lovely and lingering with a little bitterness coming through.

Domaine de Chaberton Estates 1997 Botrytis Affected Ortega
Fraser Valley VQA $26.50 (983361)
Pale amber in colour, the wine's initial impression is minerally, earthy and nutty with hints of bitter orange. The palate is quite strong, warm, perfumed, off-dry, slightly bitter and full-bodied. The orange peel and warmth sit on the tongue and the finish is long and lingering.

Hillebrand Estates 1998 Showcase Special Select Late Harvest Vidal
Ontario VQA $17.95 (000794)
Intense aromas of apricot and peach dominate the nose, while peach flavours persist on the palate of this mouth-filling wine. A slight bitterness on the finish adds some complexity.

Peller Estates 1997 Founder's Series Late Harvest Vidal
Ontario VQA $12.95 (395814)
Smoky peach flavours and some nutty notes are featured in this finely structured dessert wine. A lighter late harvest, this is a food-friendly wine that will enhance a simple dessert of fresh fruit, lemon flan or rice pudding.

Pillitteri Estates Winery 1997 Select Late Harvest Gewürztraminer/Riesling
Niagara Peninsula VQA $24.95 (435701)
A pronounced nose of rose petals, chamomile, lychee and citrus fruit combines with a slightly sweet palate. Elegant and alluring, this winning vintage is lively and quite delicious.

Reif Estates Winery 1998 Select Late Harvest Chardonnay

Niagara Peninsula VQA $19.95

The panel was struck by this wine's interesting nose of marzipan (sweet almond) and citrus. The palate is full, semi-sweet, nutty with some bitterness, lively (good acidity) and has a reasonable length. Treat your friends and family to a new flavour sensation with this stylish sweet wine.

Wild Goose Vineyards 1998 Late Harvest Riesling

Okanagan Valley VQA $12.95 (434308)

The pronounced nose of aged Riesling features petrol and diesel, almonds and little fruit other than lemon-lime. The palate is light, lively (quite crisp acidity) and citrusy, and the finish is short. This one exhibits a very different style from the majority of late harvest wines we tasted in that it is light and has little sweetness.

REFERENCE SOURCES FOR CANADIAN WINES

BOOKS

Vintage Canada:
The Complete Guide to Canadian Wines, 3rd edition
by Tony Aspler
McGraw-Hill Ryerson, 1999

Chardonnay and Friends:
Varietal Wines of British Columbia
by John Schreiner
Orca Book Publishers, 1999

Canadian Wine for Dummies
by Tony Aspler and Barbara Leslie
CDG Books Canada, 2000

Touring Niagara's Wine Country
by Linda Bramble
James Lorimer & Co., 2000

Oxford Companion to the Wines of North America
edited by Bruce Cass, with
consultant editor, Jancis Robinson
Oxford University Press, 2000

MAGAZINES

Vines Magazine
159 York Street, St. Catharines,
  ON L2R 6E9
Toll-free 1-888-883-3372
Telephone 905-682-4509
www.vinesmag.com
For a free copy of *Vines*, contact us.

Wine Access
162 John Street, Third Floor,
  Toronto, ON M5V 2E5.
Telephone: 416-596-1555
Fax: 416-596-1520
www.wineaccessmag.com

BC Wine Trails
P.O. Box 1319, Summerland, BC
  V08 1Z0
Telephone: 250-494-7733
Fax: 250-494-7737
www.bcwine.com/trails

WEB SITES

www.canwine.com
www.vancouver-island-bc.com/canadianwines
www.wineroute.com
www.winesofcanada.com
www.bcwine.com
www.brocku.ca/ccovi
www.winegrowers.bc.ca

CANADIAN WINERY INDEX

British Columbia

VANCOUVER ISLAND

Alderlea Vineyards
1751 Stamps Rd., RR 1, Duncan
tel.: 250-746-7122
fax: 250-746-7122

Blue Grouse Vineyards and Winery
4365 Blue Grouse Rd., Duncan
tel.: 250-743-3834
fax: 250-743-9305
e-mail: skiltz@islandnet.com
web site:
   www.bluegrousevineyards.com

Château Wolff
2534 Maxey Rd., Nanaimo
tel.: 250-753-9669
fax: 250-753-0614

Cherry Point Vineyards
840 Cherry Point Rd., RR 3,
   Cobble Hill
tel.: 250-743-1272
fax: 250-743-1059
e-mail: ulrich@islandnet.com
web site:
   www.cherrypointvineyards.com

Saturna Island Vineyards
8 Quarry Trail, Saturna Island
tel.: 1-877-918-3388
fax: 250-539-3515
e-mail:
   wine@saturnavineyards.com
web site:
   www.saturnavineyards.com

Venturi-Schulze Vineyards
4235 Trans-Canada Hwy., RR 1,
   Cobble Hill
tel.: 250-743-5630
fax: 250-743-5638
e-mail: info@venturischulze.com
web site: www.venturischulze.com

FRASER VALLEY

Andrés Wines
2120 Vintner St., Port Moody
tel.: 604-937-3411
fax: 604-937-5487

Domaine de Chaberton Estates
1064 216th St., Langley
tel.: 1-888-332-9463
fax: 604-533-9687
e-mail: cviolet@direct.ca
web site:
   www.domainedechaberton.com

OKANAGAN VALLEY

Black Hill Estate Winery
30880 Black Sage Rd., RR 1,
    S52, C22, Oliver
tel.: 250-498-0666
fax: 250-498-0666
e-mail: info@blackhillswinery.com
web site:
    www.blackhillswinery.com

Burrowing Owl Estate Winery
100 Burrowing Owl Place, RR 1,
    S52, C20, Oliver
tel.: 1-877-498-0620
fax: 250-498-0621
e-mail: info@bovwine.com

Calona Vineyards
1125 Richter St., Kelowna
tel.: 1-888-246-4472
fax: 250-762-2999
e-mail: wineboutique@cascadia.ca

CedarCreek Estate Winery
5445 Lakeshore Rd., Kelowna
tel.:250-764-8866
fax: 250-764-2603
e-mail: info@cedarcreek.bc.ca
web site: www.cedarcreek.bc.ca

Domaine Combret
131st St. N./Road 13, Box 1170,
    Oliver
tel.: 250-498-8878
fax: 250-498-8879
e-mail:
    domaine_combret@telus.net

Gehringer Brothers Estate Winery
Road 8, RR 1, S23, C4, Oliver
tel.: 250-498-3537
fax: 250-498-3510

Gray Monk Estate Winery
1055 Camp Rd., Okanagan Centre
tel.: 1-800-663-4205
fax: 250-766-3390
e-mail: mailbox@graymonk.com
web site: www.graymonk.com

Hawthorne Mountain Vineyards
Green Lake Rd., Box 480,
    Okanagan Falls
tel.: 250-497-8267
fax: 250-497-8073
e-mail: info@hmvineyard.com
web site: www.hmvineyard.com

Hester Creek Estate Winery
13163 326th St., Box 1605, Oliver
tel.: 250-498-4435
fax: 250-498-0651
e-mail: info@hestercreek.com
web site: www.hestercreek.com

Hillside Estate Winery
1350 Naramata Rd., Penticton
tel.: 1-888-923-9463
fax: 250-493-6294
web site: www.hillsideestate.com

Inniskillin Okanagan Vineyards
Road 11 West, RR 1, S24, C5, Oliver
tel.: 1-800-498-6211
fax: 250-498-4566
web site: www.inniskillin.com

Jackson-Triggs Vintners
Highway 97, PO Box 1650, Oliver
tel.: 250-498-4981
fax: 250-498-6505
web site: www.atlaswine.com

Lang Vineyards Ltd.
2493 Gammon Rd., RR 1, S11,
  C55, Naramata
tel.: 250-496-5987
fax: 250-496-5706

Larch Hills Winery
110 Timms Rd., Salmon Arm
tel.: 250-832-0155
fax: 250-832-9419
e-mail:
  info@LarchHillsWinery.bc.ca
web site:
  www.larchhillswinery.bc.ca

Mission Hill Estate Winery
1730 Mission Hill, Westbank
tel.: 250-768-7611
fax: 250-768-2267
e-mail: info@missionhillwinery.com
web site: www.missionhillwinery.com

Nichol Vineyard
1285 Smethurst Rd., RR 1, S14,
  C13, Naramata
tel.: 250-496-5962
fax: 250-496-4275

Paradise Ranch Vineyards
Naramata Road, Naramata
tel.: 604-683-6040
fax: 604-683-8611
e-mail: info@icewines.com

Pinot Reach Cellars
1670 Dehart Rd., Kelowna
tel.: 250-764-0078
fax: 250-764-0771
e-mail: pinot@direct.ca

Quails' Gate Estate Winery
3303 Boucherie Rd., Kelowna
tel.: 250-769-4451
fax: 250-769-245
e-mail: info@quailsgate.com
web site: www.quailsgate.com

Red Rooster Winery
910 Debeck Rd., Naramata
tel.: 250-496-4041
fax: 250-496-5674
e-mail: redrooster@img.net

St. Hubertus Estate Winery
5225 Lakeshore Rd., Kelowna
tel.: 1-800-989-9463
fax: 250-764-0499
e-mail: wine@st-hubertus.bc.ca
web site: www.st-hubertus.bc.ca

Sumac Ridge Estate Winery
Highway 97, PO Box 307,
  Summerland
tel.: 250-494-0451
fax: 250-494-3456
e-mail: sumac@vip.net
web site: www.sumacridge.com

Summerhill Estate Winery
4870 Chute Lake Rd., Kelowna
tel.: 1-800-667-3538
fax: 250-764-2598
e-mail: summerhill@summerhill.bc.ca
web site: www.summerhill.bc.ca

Tinhorn Creek Vineyards
32830 Tinhorn Creek Rd.,
  PO Box 2010, Oliver
tel.: 1-888-4-Tinhorn
fax: 250-498-3228
e-mail: winery@tinhorn.com
web site: www.tinhorn.com

Wild Goose Vineyards
2145 Sun Valley Way, RR1, S3,
  C11, Okanagan Falls
tel.: 250-497-8919
fax: 250-497-6853
e-mail: wildgoose@img.net

ONTARIO

NIAGARA PENINSULA

Andrés Wines
697 South Service Rd., Grimsby
tel.: 1-800-836-3555
fax: 905-643-4944

Birchwood Estate
4676 Cherry Ave., Vineland
tel.: 905-562-8463
fax: 905-562-6344
e-mail: agreen@diamondwines.com
web site: www.birchwoodwines.com

Cave Spring Cellars
3836 Main St., Jordan
tel.: 905-562-3581
fax: 905-562-3232
e-mail:
  cscwine@cavespringcellars.com
web site:
  www.cavespringcellars.com

Château des Charmes Estate Winery
1025 York Rd., Niagara-on-the-
  Lake
tel.: 905-262-4219
fax: 905-262-5548
e-mail:
  info@chateaudescharmes.com
web site:
  www.chateaudescharmes.com

Creekside Estate Winery
2170 4th Ave., Jordan Station
tel.: 1-877-262-9463
fax: 905-562-5493
web site:
  www.creeksideestatewinery.com

Crown Bench Estates Winery
3850 Aberdeen Rd., Beamsville
tel.: 905-563-3959
fax: 905-563-3441
e-mail:
  winery@crownbenchestates.com
web site:
  www.crownbenchestates.com

Daniel Lenko Estate Winery
5246 Regional Road 81,
  Beamsville
tel.: 905-563-7756
fax: 905-563-3317
e-mail: oldvines@DanielLenko.com
web site: www.daniellenko.com

DeSousa Wine Cellars
3753 Quarry Rd., RR 2, Beamsville
tel.: 905-563-7269
fax: 905-338-9404
e-mail:
  desousa@desousawines.com
web site: www.desousawines.com

EastDell Estates
4041 Locust Lane, Beamsville
tel.: 905-563-9463
fax: 905-563-4633
e-mail: winery@eastdell.com
web site: www.eastdell.com

Harbour Estates Winery
4362 Jordan Rd., Jordan Station
tel.: 1-877-439-9463
fax: 905-562-3829
e-mail: info@hewwine.com
web site: www.hewwine.com

Harvest Estate Wines
1179 4th Ave., St. Catharines
tel.: 905-684-3300
e-mail: wine@vaxxine.com

Henry of Pelham Family Estate Winery
1469 Pelham Rd., St. Catharines
tel.: 905-684-8423
fax: 905-684-8444
e-mail:
    winery@henryofpelham.com
web site:
    www.henryofpelham.com

Hernder Estate Winery
1607 8th Ave., St. Catharines
tel.: 905-684-3300
fax: 905-684-3303
e-mail: wine@vaxxine.com
web site: www.hernder.com

Hillebrand Estates Winery
1249 Niagara Stone Rd., Highway
    55, RR 2, Niagara-on-the-Lake
tel.: 1-800-582-8412
e-mail: info@hillebrand.com
web site: www.hillebrand.com

Inniskillin Wines
Niagara Parkway at Line 3, RR 1,
    Niagara-on-the-Lake
tel.: 905-468-3554
fax: 905-468-5355
e-mail: inniskil@inniskillin.com
web site: www.inniskillin.com

Jackson-Triggs Winery
2145 Niagara Stone Rd., Highway
    55, Niagara-on-the-Lake
tel.: 905-564-3003
e-mail:
    info@jacksontriggswinery.com
web site:
    www.jacksontriggswinery.com

Joseph's Estate Winery
1811 Niagara Stone Rd., Highway
    55, RR 3, Niagara-on-the-Lake
tel.: 905-468-1259
fax: 905-468-9242
e-mail:
    info@josephsestatewines.com
web site:
    www.josephsestatewines.com

Kacaba Vineyards
3550 King St., Vineland
tel.: 905-562-5625
fax: 416-361-1776
web site:
    www.kacabavineyards.com

Kittling Ridge Estate Wines and Spirits
297 South Service Rd., Grimsby
tel.: 905-945-9225
fax: 905-945-4330
e-mail: admin@kittlingridge.com
web site: www.kittlingridge.com

Konzelmann Estate Winery

1696 Lakeshore Rd.,
  Niagara-on-the-Lake
tel.: 905-935-2866
fax: 905-935-2864
e-mail:
  wine@konzelmannwines.com
web site:
  www.konzelmannwines.com

Lakeview Cellars Estate Winery

4037 Cherry Ave., Vineland
tel.: 905-562-5685
fax: 905-562-0673
e-mail:
  lakecell@lakeviewcellars.on.ca
web site:
  www.lakeviewcellars.on.ca

Magnotta Winery

4701 Ontario St., Beamsville
tel.: 905-563-5313
fax: 905-738-5551
e-mail: info@magnotta.com
web site: www.magnotta.com

Maleta Vineyards

450 Queenston Rd., RR
  Niagara-on-the-Lake
tel.: 605-685-8486
fax: 905-685-7998;

Malivoire Wine Company

4260 King St. E. (Regional
  Road 81), Beamsville
tel.: 905-563-9253
fax: 905-563-9512
e-mail:
  ladybug@malivoirewineco.com
web site:
  www.malivoirewineco.com

Marynissen Estates

RR 6, Concession 1,
  Niagara-on-the-Lake
tel.: 905-468-7270
fax: 905-468-5784
web site:
  www.marynissenestates. com

Peller Estates Winery

290 John St., Niagara-on-the-Lake
tel.: 1-888-673-5537
e-mail: info@pellar.com
web site: www.peller.com

Peninsula Ridge Estates Winery

5600 King St. W. (Regional
  Road 81), Beamsville
tel.: 905-563-0900
fax: 905-563-0995
e-mail: info@peninsularidge.com
web site:
  www.peninsularidge.com

Pillitteri Estates Winery

696 Hwy. 55, RR 2, Niagara-on-
  the-Lake
tel.: 905-468-3147
fax: 905-468-0389
e-mail: winery@pillitteri.com
web site: www.pillitteri.com

Reif Estate Winery

15608 Niagara Parkway, RR 1,
  Niagara-on-the-Lake
tel.: 905-468-7738
fax: 905-468-5878
e-mail: wine@reifwinery.com
web site: www.reifwinery.com

Royal DeMaria Wines
4551 Cherry Ave., Vineland
tel.: 905-562-6767
fax: 905-562-6775
e-mail:
    icewine@royaldemaria.com
web site: www.royaldemaria.com

Stonechurch Vineyards
1270 Irvine Rd., RR 5,
    Niagara-on-the-Lake
tel.: 905-935-3535
fax: 905-646-8892
e-mail: wine@stonechurch.com
web site: www.stonechurch.com

Stoney Ridge Estate Cellars
3201 King St. (Regional Rd. 81),
    Vineland
tel.: 905-562-1324
fax: 905-562-7777
e-mail: srcellar@vaxxine.com
web site: www.stoneyridge.com

Strewn Winery
1339 Lakeshore Rd.,
    Niagara-on-the-Lake
tel.: 905-468-1229
fax: 905-468-8305
e-mail: info@strewnwinery.com
web site: www.strewnwinery.com

Thirteenth Street Wine Co.
RR 1, 13th St. S., Jordan Station
tel.: 905-562-5900
fax: 905-562-5900
e-mail: funkwine@vaxxine.com

Thirty Bench Wines
4281 Mountainview Rd.,
    Beamsville
tel.: 905-563-1698
fax: 905-563-392
e-mail: wine@thirtybench.com
web site: www.thirtybench.com

Thomas & Vaughan Vintners
4245 King St. (Regional Road 81),
    Beamsville
tel.: 905-563-7737
fax: 905-563-4114
e-mail:
    info@thomasandvaughan.com
web site:
    www.thomasandvaughan.com

Vineland Estates Winery
3620 Moyer Rd., RR 1, Vineland
tel.: 905-562-7088
fax: 905-562-3071
e-mail: wine@vineland.com
web site: www.vineland.com

Willow Heights Winery
3751 Regional Road 81, RR 1,
    Vineland
tel.: 905-562-4945
fax: 905-562-5761
e-mail:
    willow.heights@sympatico.ca
web site: www.willowheights.on.ca

LAKE ERIE NORTH SHORE

Colio Estate Wines
1 Colio Dr., Harrow
tel.: 1-800-265-1322
fax: 519-738-3070
e-mail: colio@total.net
web site: www.colio.com

D'Angelo Estate Winery
5141 Concession 5, RR 4,
  Amherstburg
tel.: 519-736-7959
fax: 519-736-1912
e-mail:
  dangelowines@on.aibn.com

Pelee Island Winery
455 Seacliff Dr., Kingsville
tel.: 1-800-597-3533
e-mail: pelee@peleeisland.com
web site: www.peleeisland.com

TORONTO

Cilento Wines
672 Chrislea Rd., Woodbridge
tel.: 1-888-245-9463
e-mail: cilento@ica.net
web site: www.cilento.com

Southbrook Farm and Winery
1061 Major Mackenzie Dr., Maple
tel.: 905-832-2548
e-mail: office@southbrook.com
web site: www.southbrook.com